The Church and Pastoral Care

Psychology and Christianity
Edited by David G. Benner

The Church and Pastoral Care

Edited by

LEROY ADEN
J. HAROLD ELLENS

BAKER BOOK HOUSE
Grand Rapids, Michigan 49516

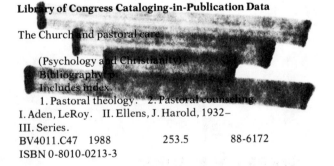

Library of Congress Cataloging-in-Publication Data

The Church and pastoral care.

   (Psychology and Christianity)
   Bibliography: p.
   Includes index.
   1. Pastoral theology.   2. Pastoral counseling.
I. Aden, LeRoy.   II. Ellens, J. Harold, 1932–
III. Series.
BV4011.C47   1988   253.5   88-6172
ISBN 0-8010-0213-3

Contents

Introduction to the Series

Psychology and Christianity is a series of books published cooperatively by Baker Book House and the Christian Association for Psychological Studies (CAPS). Founded in 1952 in Grand Rapids, Michigan, by a group of psychologists, psychiatrists, and pastoral counselors, CAPS is an international society of Christian helping-professionals committed to the exploration of the relationship between psychology and Christian faith.

Books in this series draw on CAPS publications, many of which are now out of print. From 1952 to 1974 the organization published the proceedings of its annual conventions. Then it replaced these proceedings with a quarterly professional journal, *The Bulletin of CAPS*, which in turn was replaced by the *Journal of Psychology and Christianity* in 1982.

This monograph series will present psychological and theological reflection on basic issues encountered in helping, ministry, parenting, and educational relationships. After *Christian Counseling and Psychotherapy*, volumes in the series will include *Life-Span Growth and Development; Sin, Guilt, and Forgiveness; Psychospiritual Health and Pathology;* and *Personality and Biblical Anthropology.*

Further information about the Christian Association for Psychological Studies may be obtained from the head office:

Christian Association for Psychological Studies
26705 Farmington Road
Farmington Hills, Michigan 48018
(313) 477–1350

David G. Benner
Series Editor

Contributors

LeRoy Aden is Luther D. Reed Professor of Pastoral Care at the Lutheran Theological Seminary, Philadelphia, Pennsylvania.

Herbert Anderson is a pastor of the Lutheran church and professor of pastoral care at the Catholic Theological Union, Chicago, Illinois.

Donald Capps is professor of pastoral theology at Princeton Theological Seminary, Princeton, New Jersey.

Thomas A. Droege is professor of theology at Valparaiso University, Valparaiso, Indiana.

J. Harold Ellens is executive director of the Christian Association for Psychological Studies and is editor-in-chief of the *Journal of Psychology and Christianity.*

James M. Gustafson is University Professor of Ethics at the University of Chicago, Chicago, Illinois.

Lyman T. Lundeen is Ministerium of New York Professor of Systematic Theology at the Lutheran Theological Seminary, Philadelphia, Pennsylvania.

Thomas C. Oden is Henry Anson Buttz Professor of Theology at the Theological School, Drew University, Madison, New Jersey.

Lewis B. Smedes is professor of theology and ethics at Fuller Theological Seminary, Pasadena, California.

Introduction

Protestant pastoral care is alive and well. Theological students in increasing numbers are supplementing their academic diets in the seminary with the rich fiber of clinically supervised ministry to persons. Doctor of Ministry programs are attracting more candidates than most departments of pastoral care can handle, and parish pastors are called upon to give pastoral care and counseling to a growing number of troubled people in a plethora of circumstances.

Fortunately, those who are involved in the theory and practice of pastoral care are not complacent. On the contrary, there is a growing desire to get pastoral care and counseling back to its roots, a need to reestablish it as a vital dimension of the Christian faith and an essential function of Christian ministry. In part, the need comes from a good thing that has been taken too far—the use of the psychological sciences to illumine the pastoral task. Modern psychology, beginning with Sigmund Freud, has made a great and undeniable contribution to pastoral care, but many of us in the field became so enamored by the findings of psychology that we neglected the essentially theological nature of pastoral ministry. We were impressed with an impressive fact—the ability of therapeutic psychology to lay bare the profound reaches of human existence, its struggle with fear and anxiety, guilt and shame, life and death. This ability still deserves respect, but when psychology becomes a dominant and determinative orientation it robs pastoral care of its distinctiveness and makes it a pseudopsychiatric enterprise. In a word, it tends to psychologize pastoral care out of the church.

The move back to theological foundations is well under way. Clinical pastoral educators, who once were in the forefront of the move toward psychology, are regaining a serious interest in theology. And in the last fifteen years theorists in the field have taken a firm hold of the role of theology in pastoral concerns. Seward Hiltner led the way by exploring how "theology, understood dynamically, illumines psychology, and is in turn enriched by dynamic psychology."[1] Wayne E. Oates reversed the direction but deepened our understanding of the faith by bringing a "comprehensive psychological approach to the study of religious experience."[2] Meanwhile, Don S. Browning brought fresh air to the theory and practice of pastoral care by challenging us to take its moral context seriously. More recently, men like William B. Oglesby, Jr., and Donald Capps have been adventurous enough to consider the methods and the process of pastoral care and counseling from a biblical perspective.[3]

This monograph continues and, we hope, extends the discussion. It is an expanded and revised version of the winter 1984 issue of the *Journal of Psychology and Christianity*, which focused on pastoral issues; that is, on theoretical and practical concerns that are raised by, or that are relevant to, the practice of counseling in the church. Each author is attentive to the theological dimensions of pastoral care and makes a significant contribution to its clarification from his own particular vantage point. The result is a rich menu of articles on major dimensions of the church's pastoral ministry.

The first three chapters deal with foundational concerns, seeking to clarify the basic orientation of pastoral care as a ministry of the church.

Thomas C. Oden begins the discussion. From an attempt in the 1950s "to effect a workable integration" of Carl R. Rogers's therapy of self-disclosure with Karl Barth's theology of divine self-disclosure, Oden has come through various stages to a point where he is concerned "to recover the classical pastoral tradition" of the church in order to enrich contemporary pastoral care and counseling. After showing that pastoral care has indeed ignored the classical tradition, he constructs a heuristic list of changes that might occur in the orientation of pastoral care if it were to reconnect with its heritage.

In chapter 2, LeRoy Aden follows Oden's lead by elaborating a theological understanding of both the task and the source of pastoral care. The task is defined in light of the church's responsibility to pro-

1. Seward Hiltner, *Theological Dynamics* (Nashville: Abingdon, 1972), 14.

2. Wayne E. Oates, *The Psychology of Religion* (Waco: Word, 1973).

3. Don S. Browning, *The Moral Context of Pastoral Care* (Philadelphia: Westminster, 1976); William B. Oglesby, Jr., *Biblical Themes for Pastoral Care* (Nashville: Abingdon, 1980); Donald Capps, *Biblical Approaches to Pastoral Counseling* (Philadelphia: Westminster, 1981).

claim the Word; the source is located in our response of love to what God is and does for us in Christ. Clarification of these foundational concerns, however important, should not be confused with the daily operation of pastoral care. What we often see in practice is not the theological underpinnings of pastoral care, but its persistent focus on the situation of the needy person and its attempt to understand and to relate to that situation by using the resources of content and method that we have learned from the human sciences. This focus is not a shift away from the gospel but an extension of it, for God's Good News sends us to needy neighbors to love and to serve according to their specific needs.

In previous publications, Donald Capps has elucidated the goals of pastoral care by studying the literary forms of the Bible. In chapter 3, he reviews the ways in which the Bible has been used in pastoral care and counseling from 1930 to the present. Out of this historical sketch he identifies four principles that need to be taken seriously if the Bible is to be an effective resource in pastoral ministry.

Herbert Anderson starts a trilogy of chapters in which pastoral counseling is brought into conversation with particular theological concepts.

Beginning with the theological affirmation that in Christ the divine is embodied in the human, Anderson examines four ways in which the metaphor of incarnation has been applied to pastoral care. He finds that in each case the metaphor is helpful in illuminating the identity of either the care-giver or the one being cared for, but he also finds definite limitations with the application and warns that we should not make the incarnation of God too dependent on our own care-giving. He reminds us that God's care is active in the world, whether or not our particular form of care giving incarnates it.

Lewis B. Smedes's penetrating study of forgiveness is both theological and practical in the best sense of those words. It is theological in the sense that it bases our ability to forgive on the gift of divine forgiveness that we have received; it is practical in the sense that it sheds light on some of the dynamics involved in the act of forgiving. Smedes's discussion should be helpful to any care-giver, whether lay or ordained.

The sixth chapter considers forgiveness from a different perspective. Setting it in dialectical relation to fulfillment as an end point of pastoral care and counseling, this chapter argues that a Christian understanding of the human condition, at least a Pauline one, suggests that forgiveness, and not fulfillment, addresses and answers our deepest restlessness.

Chapters 7 and 8 are concerned with the moral dimension of pastoral counseling.

James M. Gustafson brings the perspective of a Protestant ethicist to the discussion. He suggests that moral counseling is an important but often neglected aspect of pastoral care. By moral counseling, he means a pastoral relationship in which questions of "What ought I to do?" are primary. He suggests that moral counseling proceeds primarily by way of interrogation, not in an invasive or authoritarian way but in a dialogic way where the total situation of the person is investigated and clarified in order to help him or her come to an appropriate ethical decision.

Chapter 8 then brings the data of a pastoral counselor to the discussion and tries to clarify the points at which effective counseling seems to bring about moral change in the individual. Here it is suggested that the change is related to, or actually is a part of, a larger pattern of growth that occurs in the individual's personal and interpersonal life. In this sense, counseling serves as an instrument of significant change, moving the individual beyond mere obedience to external law toward the fulfillment of his or her God-given personhood in a community of persons.

Faith is the common coinage of the next three chapters as they deal in turn with conversion, growth in faith, and death.

J. Harold Ellens adopts the developmental insight that adults grow or change as a result of paradigmatic events. He identifies Christian conversion as such an event and investigates its psychodynamics. He finds that it can be either pathogenic (a reinforcement of neurotic tendencies) or health-producing (a genuine reintegration of the personality), depending on the degree to which it represents an unconditional acceptance of God's proffered grace rather than an abortive attempt to justify ourselves.

Thomas A. Droege, whose study of faith from a developmental point of view predates much of the current literature on the subject, deals with the relation between pastoral counseling and faith developmental theory. He maintains that while pastoral counseling has tended theologically to emphasize pathology or sin, faith developmental theory has tended to emphasize growth or sanctification. He shows that each perspective can enhance the other, that in fact neither one is complete without the other.

Lyman T. Lundeen deals with the church's ministry to the dying and the bereaved. He brings the perspective of a systematic theologian to the task and explores five crucial ways in which faith relates to death. Over against a reductionistic perspective that maintains that faith silences death and makes all our sorrows go away, he shows that the Christian faith helps us to acknowledge the full tragedy of death, even as it provides sufficient resources to deal with it. Speaking from the vantage point of Christ's incarnation into our lives, he maintains that it is in taking our concrete situation more, rather than less, seriously that we experience life in the midst of death, hope in the midst of despair.

Work with marital partners and families is a vital part of the church's care. In the twelfth chapter, Herbert Anderson, who has recently published a study of *The Family and Pastoral Care*, explores the idea that individuals within families, and therefore families themselves, change.[4] He identifies five epochs in a family's life cycle and maintains that in each epoch the family has a "developmental task" to achieve. He completes his discussion by clarifying some of the major impediments to the achievement of each task and by pointing to some of the resources that the church has to help families meet the challenge of change.

The next chapter discusses the reality of change in a larger context, specifically in our contemporary social scene where there is tension between men and women, husbands and wives, blacks and whites. The first section uses Paul Tillich's discussion of anxiety to clarify the level at which we are often threatened by significant social change. This is followed by a challenge to care in the midst of change by seeing ourselves for what we are—finite and limited creatures. Lessons that our mortality can teach us, especially if we acknowledge our finitude before God, are then developed.

In the final chapter, LeRoy Aden uses Ernest Becker's profound understanding of the human condition to call for a new approach to pastoral care. Becker maintains that the human predicament is part of our own making. If he is right, pastoral care must not only comfort us in our affliction but also afflict us in our comfortableness. The art of pastoral counseling is to know the difference between the two and to be able to mediate each at the appropriate time and in an effective way.

As a concluding comment, we wish to thank each author for his contribution to this volume. Building on the work of people who have contributed to contemporary pastoral theory, each writer extends our understanding of pastoral care and counseling. We hope this increased understanding multiplies our ability to help those in need, not only in terms of their relationship to self and others but also in terms of their relationship to God. In the past four or five decades, pastoral care has been attentive to psychological dynamics. In the last ten years, it has gained a new awareness of the moral context of caring. Unfortunately, it has been less conscientious, and certainly less systematic, about its theological orientation, even though pastoral care as part of the church's

---

4. Herbert Anderson, *The Family and Pastoral Care* (Philadelphia: Fortress, 1984).

ministry is basically a theological, and not a psychological or a moral, enterprise. The authors in this volume are attentive to that fact. They do not all operate out of the same theological framework, but they all appreciate the priority of a theological perspective. That is why they present perceptive inquiries into dimensions of pastoral care and counseling that are relevant to the healing of the human spirit. That is why their endeavors represent a significant attempt to reestablish pastoral care as a vital dimension of the Christian faith and as an essential function of Christian ministry.

The authors wish to acknowledge the work of Linda Triemstra, a senior copy editor at Baker Book House, in reading proofs and indexing.

1

Recovering Pastoral Care's Lost Identity

Thomas C. Oden

A major effort is needed today to rediscover and remine the classical models of Christian pastoral care and to make available once again the key texts of that classical tradition following about fifty years of neglect, the depths of which are arguably unprecedented in any previous Christian century. A whole generation of pastoral scholars will be needed to recover textually and rediscover practically the classics of pastoral care, texts that reach out for the contemporary working pastor in the counseling task. [*Care of Souls in the Classic Tradition*] presents one such patristic voice, Gregory the Great, as an exemplar of classical pastoral care, but there are many others whose works need to find their way back to contemporary pastoral practice.

Classical Pastoral Care: A Textual Definition

Many of the key classical sources that have carried enormous weight for centuries of Christian pastoral counseling are available now only from rare book sources. Pastors and religious counselors today are hungering for deeper rootage in a tradition that is in many cases not even available to them.

The identification of the classical style of Christian pastoral care is best achieved by pointing to a series of venerable texts that have been repeatedly and resourcefully used as key reference points for the church's pastoral ministry, many of them steadily for over a millennium. These texts begin essentially with the New Testament pastoral and catholic Epistles and continue through many stages of development—patristic, medieval, and Reformation—well into the nineteenth century, where pastoral theologians as varied as Horace Bushnell, Alexandre Vinet, and Washington Gladden demonstrate that the tradition was diligently remembered and often quoted.

Although this is a richly varied body of literature, I will mention only a few of the most widely quoted sources that have often carried the essential burden of the tradition. Our purpose at this point is to show in a preliminary way that there is in fact a classical pastoral tradition and that this tradition is embodied in a well-defined series of texts: Cyprian's writings on patience, jealousy, and envy; Tertullian's works on the soul; Chrysostom on the priesthood; Ambrose on the responsibilities of the clergy; and numerous works by Augustine— on the soul, happiness, admonition, patience, and grief counseling.

At the center of the pastoral tradition is Gregory's *Pastoral Care,* which for more than a millennium was considered to be the indispensable guide to pastoral counseling; followed by Bonaventure on the right ordering of the soul; various sections of Thomas Aquinas's *Summa Theologica* on happiness, fear, anger, the emotions, the dispositions, love, and desire; Hugh of St. Victor on preparation for confession, anointing of the sick, and care for the dying.

The Reformation tradition of pastoral care is seen in Martin Luther's table-talk and letters; Zwingli on the pastor; John Calvin's letters; Martin Bucer on visitation of the sick and poor; Thomas More's prison writings; George Herbert's *Country Parson;* Gilbert Burnet's discourse on pastoral care; Jeremy Taylor's spiritual exercises; Richard Baxter on self-acquaintance; the astute English tradition of pastoral direction represented by Anglican bishops Wilson, Spratt, Gibson, and Hort; many eighteenth-century writers such as Philip Doddridge, Count Nicolas von Zinzendorf, Jonathan Edwards, John Wesley, and William Paley, who were all interested in pastoral care and the caring community.

They were followed by the pivotal contributions to the study of practical theology by F. D. Schleiermacher, J. M. Sailer, Claus Harms, Wilhelm Loehe, H. A. Koestlin, J. B. Renninger, Theodosius Harnack, J. T. Beck, and Carl Immanuel Nitzsch in the nineteenth-century German tradition. In the English tradition J. H. Newman, F. D. Maurice, Charles Bridges, and Handley Moule made key contributions, while the Swiss Protestant tradition was wisely represented by Alexandre Vinet.[1]

The preliminary list could be much longer, but at least this will serve to show where some of the basic textual materials lie for the restudy and redefinition of pastoral counseling today, lost as it appears now to be in what [Erik H.] Erikson would call an "identity diffusion."[2] Although there are fascinating varieties within this tradition, a careful examination will show that it is indeed a single developing tradition rather than a plethora of unrelated traditions. It is unified by its eucharistic center and its concern to embody the living Christ through interpersonal meeting.

Recent Clinical Pastoral Counseling: Has Pastoral Identity Been Misplaced?

What curious fate has befallen the classical tradition of pastoral care in the last five decades? It has been steadily accommodated to a series of psychotherapies. It has fallen deeply into a pervasive amnesia toward its own classical pastoral past, into a vague absent-mindedness about the great figures of this distinguished tradition, and into what can only generously be called a growing ignorance of classical pastoral care.

In order to test out my hypothesis that the classical pastoral tradition has been quickly and abruptly forgotten in the twentieth century, I gathered some data from the indexes of leading books on pastoral theology from the nineteenth and twentieth centuries. I selected ten key figures in classical pastoral care that seemed to carry the tradition most significantly: Cyprian, Tertullian, Chrysostom, Augustine, Gregory the Great, Luther, Calvin, George Herbert, Richard Baxter, and Jeremy Taylor. I then checked out the number of times they were referred to in seven standard works of pastoral theology in the nineteenth century, those by William G. T. Shedd of Union (Presbyterian),[3]

---

1. For a more complete bibliography of the classics of the pastoral tradition, please refer to the twelve hundred or so entries in the bibliography of Thomas C. Oden, *Pastoral Theology: Essentials of Ministry* (San Francisco: Harper and Row, 1983), 317–54. Regrettably a large number of these books are out of print. The purpose in setting forth this modest preliminary list is to help the reader to become aware that there is a definite body of important pastoral texts once widely known but now largely neglected.

2. Erik H. Erikson, *Identity and the Life Cycle* (New York: International Universities Press, 1959), chapters 2 and 3.

3. William G. T. Shedd, *Homiletics and Pastoral Theology* (New York: Charles Scribner's Sons, 1867).

Patrick Fairbairn of Glasgow (Scottish Presbyterian),[4] James M. Hoppin of Yale (Congregationalist),[5] Charles Bridges (Church of England),[6] Heinrich Koestlin of Giessen (Lutheran),[7] Washington Gladden of Columbus (Congregationalist),[8] and Daniel Kidder of Drew (Methodist).[9] I found that every one of these authors unfailingly quoted Chrysostom, Augustine, Luther, Calvin, Herbert, and Baxter (table 1). There were [314] references in all to our ten classical pastoral guides. Most often referred to were [Baxter, Augustine, Luther, and Calvin, followed by Chrysostom, Herbert, Taylor, and Cyprian.] This clearly establishes the point that at the turn of the century the classical tradition was alive and well, recalled, and considered important to the practice of pastoral care.

Table 1 **Representative Nineteenth-Century Pastoral Writers: Frequency of Reference to the Classical Pastoral Tradition**

	Shedd (1879) Presbyterian	Fairbairn (1875) Scottish Presbt.	Hoppin (1884) Congregationalist	Bridges (1829) Church of England	Koestlin (1895) Lutheran	Gladden (1891) Congregationalist	Kidder (1871) Methodist	Total
Cyprian	—	1	1	6	2	—	1	11
Tertullian	2	1	2	1	1	—	—	7
Chrysostom	1	2	6	13	6	3	2	33
Augustine	9	1	1	37	2	2	1	53
Gregory	—	—	1	6	2	1	—	10
Luther	6	1	4	22	11	5	1	50
Calvin	8	1	1	25	3	2	1	41
Baxter	8	7	2	37	3	3	1	61
Herbert	1	1	4	19	1	4	1	31
Taylor	2	1	3	7	2	2	—	17
Totals	37	16	25	173	33	22	8	314

4. Patrick Fairbairn, *Pastoral Theology* (Edinburgh: T. and T. Clark, 1872).

5. James M. Hoppin, *Pastoral Theology* (New York: Funk and Wagnalls, 1884).

6. Charles Bridges, *The Christian Ministry* (New York: Carter, 1847).

7. Heinrich Koestlin, *Die Lehre von der Seelsorge* (Berlin: Reuther and Reichard, 1895).

8. Washington Gladden, *The Christian Pastor* (New York: Charles Scribner's Sons, 1898).

9. Daniel Kidder, *The Christian Pastorate* (New York: Methodist Book Concern, 1871).

Curiosity aroused, I then selected seven major contemporary writers on pastoral counseling whose influence I judged to be most general and whose views seemed by consensus to be most representative. I chose the most widely used texts of four well-known Americans—Seward Hiltner, Howard Clinebell, Wayne E. Oates, and Carroll A. Wise[10]—and three Europeans—from the Lutheran tradition Dietrich Stollberg, from the Reformed tradition Paul Tournier, and from the Roman Catholic tradition Father Joseph Nuttin of Louvain.[11] In all these major modern pastoral works I could not find even a single quotation by or reference to Augustine, Baxter, Calvin, Cyprian, Chrysostom, Gregory the Great, or Luther (table 2). It is as if for these contemporary pastoral counselors classical pastoral thought did not impinge relevantly on their work.

This further whetted my interest in seeing how many references these same current writers might be making to key modern psycholo-

Table 2 **Representative Twentieth-Century Pastoral Writers: Frequency of Reference to Classical Texts of Pastoral Care**

	Hiltner	Clinebell	Oates	Wise	Tournier	Stollberg	Nuttin	Total
Cyprian	0	0	0	0	0	0	0	0
Tertullian	0	0	0	0	0	0	0	0
Chrysostom	0	0	0	0	0	0	0	0
Augustine	0	0	0	0	0	0	0	0
Gregory	0	0	0	0	0	0	0	0
Luther	0	0	0	0	0	0	0	0
Calvin	0	0	0	0	0	0	0	0
Herbert	0	0	0	0	0	0	0	0
Baxter	0	0	0	0	0	0	0	0
Taylor	0	0	0	0	0	0	0	0
Totals	0	0	0	0	0	0	0	0

10. Seward Hiltner, *Pastoral Counseling* (Nashville: Abingdon, 1949); Howard Clinebell, *Basic Types of Pastoral Counseling* (Nashville: Abingdon, 1966); Wayne E. Oates, *Pastoral Counseling* (Philadelphia: Westminster, 1974); and Carroll A. Wise, *Pastoral Counseling* (New York: Harper, 1951).

11. Dietrich Stollberg, *Therapeutische Seelsorge* (Munich: Chr. Kaiser, 1969); Paul Tournier, *The Doctor's Casebook in the Light of the Bible* (New York: Harper, 1960); Joseph Nuttin, *Psychoanalysis and Personality* (New York: New American Library, 1962).

gists and psychotherapists in their attempt to give guidance to Christian pastoral counselors. I selected six major psychotherapeutic contributors—Freud, Jung, Rogers, Sullivan, Berne, and Fromm—and found 330 references to these modern figures in the same seven widely used texts, including 109 references to Freud, 101 to Rogers, 45 to Jung, 27 to Fromm, 26 to Berne, and 22 to Sullivan (table 3). In most cases these writers were being quoted with approval or referred to as authoritative guides for pastoral counseling.

This exercise astonished me. It provided preliminary [confirmation of] a hunch I had felt for a long time—namely, that contemporary psychotherapists are far more inwardly important and objectively authoritative for pastoral counseling today than are the writers of classical Christian pastoral care. I invite others to check this out for themselves, using different historical and contemporary writers; I think the result will be the same.

What happened after 1920? It was as if a slow pendulum gradually reversed its direction and began to swing headlong toward modern psychological accommodation. A key figure in the reversal was Anton Boisen, founder of the clinical pastoral education movement, a creative man in whom the classical tradition still lived and whose works are still eminently worth reading.[12] But after Boisen, pastoral care soon acquired a consuming interest in psychoanalysis, psychopathology, clinical methods of treatment, and in the whole string of thera-

Table 3 **Representative Twentieth-Century Pastoral Writers: Frequency of Reference to Modern Psychotherapists**

	Hiltner	Clinebell	Oates	Wise	Tournier	Stollberg	Nuttin	Total
Freud	8	8	9	1	9	5	69	109
Jung	10	6	1	—	13	3	12	45
Rogers	19	18	4	6	—	26	28	101
Fromm	8	6	—	9	—	1	3	27
Sullivan	5	4	5	5	—	1	2	22
Berne	—	19	6	—	—	1	—	26
Totals	50	61	25	21	22	37	114	330

12. Anton Boisen, *Out of the Depths* (New York: Harper, 1960).

peutic approaches that were to follow Freud.[13] It was a vital and significant task, but regrettably the theological moorings were not sufficiently deep to prevent an ever-increasing drift toward forgetfulness of the previous traditions of pastoral counseling. It is as if a giant shade had been pulled. Classic pastoral wisdom fell into a deep sleep for about four decades.

During these decades we have witnessed wave after wave of various hegemonies of emergent psychologies being accommodated, often cheaply, into pastoral care without much self-conscious identity formation from the tradition. I do not want to exaggerate so as to suggest that the classical tradition of pastoral care was entirely forgotten. That did not happen (as we can see especially in the brilliant work of Frank Lake).[14] We are still living implicitly out of the quiet influences of that vital but inconspicuous tradition. It is amazing how resilient these patterns of pastoral response can be, even when they are not being deliberately studied. For language assumptions and recurrent historical paradigms may continue to be maintained at operational levels by social traditioning, despite rapidly changing ideologies and leadership elites and the appearance of novelty. But the classical tradition has not been diligently studied since the 1920s. It has lain fallow and borne only occasional wild fruit. We are now at the far end of that pendulum swing, and the momentum is again reversing toward an emerging hunger for classical wisdom.

During the past twenty-five years of my professional life the methodological key to the active energies of pastoral care has been its pervasive hunger for the accommodation of various therapies from orthodox Freudian and Jungian all the way through the broad and colorful spectrum of Harry Stack Sullivan, Carl R. Rogers, B. F. Skinner, Erich Fromm, Fritz Perls, Eric Berne, Albert Ellis, Will Schutz, and Joseph Wolpe—all of whom one by one have been courted and welcomed and accommodated (often rather uncritically) into the practice, structures, language, and professional apparatus of Christian ministry. The task of the pastoral counselor thus understood in recent years has tended to become that of trying to ferret out what is currently happening or likely to happen next in the sphere of emergent psychologies and adapting it as deftly as possible to the work of min-

13. This history has been partially chronicled in Seward Hiltner, ed., *Clinical Pastoral Training* (New York: Federal Council of Churches, 1945); Charles Kemp, *Physicians of the Soul: A History of Pastoral Counseling* (New York: Macmillan, 1947); Edward Thornton, *Professional Education for Ministry: A History of Clinical Pastoral Education* (Nashville: Abingdon, 1969).

14. Frank Lake, *Clinical Theology* (London: Darton, Longman and Todd, 1966).

istry. In the adaptation, however, the fundament of Christian pastoral care in its classical sense has at best been neglected and at worst polemicized. So pastoral theology has become in many cases little more than a thoughtless mimic of the most current psychological trends. Often these trends, as psychologist Paul Vitz has astutely shown, have been bad psychology to begin with.[15] Modern pastoral counseling has had only the slenderest accountability to the classical pastoral tradition. Meanwhile it is little wonder that the working pastor continues to look in vain to the field of pastoral theology for some distinction between Christian pastoral care and popular psychological faddism. I may be exaggerating slightly, but I think not much.

This process might plausibly have continued further for some time to come were it not for the most damaging and embarrassing blow to such accommodationism—the studies of psychotherapeutic effectiveness. I refer to the slowly growing recognition of the fate-laden importance of the so-called outcome studies disclosing the actual results attained through application of the various psychotherapies. Slowly but surely we are finally learning more and more about the surprising ineffectiveness of average psychotherapy. An accumulation of controlled studies by highly respected psychologists (Allen Bergin, Hans Eysenck, Hans Strupp, Jerome Frank, Charles Truax, Robert Carkhuff, and Philip Hanson) has convincingly shown that the average psychotherapy cure rate is about the same as that which eventuates merely through the passage of time, approximately 65 to 70 percent.

This is not just somebody's curious idea or untested theory, but a well-supported conclusion based on over three hundred controlled empirical studies.[16] These outcome studies have caused me to question the effectiveness of the very psychotherapies upon which I had earlier been building my case as a theologian in dialogue with behavior-change theories. The evidence has been accumulating for a long time, but to date it has been almost systematically ignored by the accommodationist trend that has until recently become virtually normative in recent American pastoral care. The accommodation of pastoral care to psychotherapy has bottomed out proportionally as these empirical outcome studies have been taken seriously.

These data prompt us to return to the thornier question: Has bondage to the assumptions of modern consciousness resulted in the loss

15. Paul Vitz, *Psychology as Religion* (Grand Rapids: Eerdmans, 1977).

16. For a general review of these therapeutic effectiveness studies, see Thomas C. Oden, "A Populist's View of Psychotherapeutic Deprofessionalization," *Journal of Humanistic Psychology* (Spring 1974), and "Consumer Interests in Therapeutic Outcome Studies," *Journal of Humanistic Psychology* 15 (Summer 1975), as well as *Game Free: A Guide to the Meaning of Intimacy* (New York: Harper and Row, 1974), chapter 3.

of our freedom to learn from the classical pastoral tradition? I think the short answer, at least in the USA, is yes. The longer answer could be stated in the form of a hypothesis for further discussion: Recent pastoral counseling has incurred a fixated dependency upon and an indebtedness to modern psychology and modern consciousness generally that has prevented it from even looking at all premodern wisdoms, including classical pastoral care. This has amounted to a net loss of freedom, a harsh constriction on the freedom to learn. We have bet all our chips on the assumption that modern consciousness will lead us into vaster freedoms while our specific freedom to be attentive to our own Christian pastoral tradition has been plundered, polemicized, and despoiled.

Evidence is growing that the time is ripe for a major restudy of classical Christian pastoral counsel. The average pastor has come to a saturation point with fads. By now most have likely done the TA trip, the T-Group trip, microlabs, and perhaps some Gestalt training, as well as dabbled with psychoanalysis and/or any number of other available therapeutic strategies—client-centered, bioenergetics, Jungian, Adlerian, rational-emotive therapy, parent effectiveness training, EST, and the list goes on and on.[17] Pastors are anxiously wondering not only how most of these approaches are to be integrated into the Christian tradition (since many of them are openly contemptuous of key assumptions of Christianity) but also what their social and historical consequences will be. Early readings are not reassuring.[18] Wise pastors know there has to be a better way. They are often tired of compliantly following psychiatric clues in an era in which psychiatry itself is more and more on the defensive and at times in public disrepute. Many pastors have long suspected what the the public-opinion analysts are now verifying, that psychiatry has the lowest trust rating among all medical specializations.

It is doubly ironic that the psychologists and psychotherapists are themselves beginning to call pastors back to their traditional pastoral identity. Major statements by therapists Karl Menninger, Frank Lake, Paul W. Pruyser, O. Hobart Mowrer, Ruth Barnhouse, and Paul Vitz[19] have forcefully stated this point, and there is every reason to believe

17. See *The Intensive Group Experience* (Philadelphia: Westminster, 1972), chapters 1 and 5.

18. See chapter 1 of my discussion in *Guilt Free* (Nashville: Abingdon, 1980).

19. Karl Menninger, *Whatever Became of Sin?* (New York: Hawthorn, 1972); Lake, *Clinical Theology;* Paul W. Pruyser, *The Minister as Diagnostician* (Philadelphia: Westminster, 1976); O. Hobart Mowrer, *The Crisis in Psychiatry and Religion* (New York: Van Nostrand, 1961); Ruth Barnhouse, "Spiritual Direction and Psychotherapy," *Journal of Pastoral Care* 33 (September 1979): 149–63; Vitz, *Psychology as Religion.*

that the momentum in this direction will increase. In speaking of the religious counselors he has worked with, Paul Pruyser writes, "I became aware that much of the instruction was one-sided, with the consent of both parties: the theologians sat at the feet of the psychiatric Gamaliels and seemed to like it. Pastors were eager to absorb as much psychological knowledge and skill as they could, without even thinking of instructional reciprocity. . . . I have learned that ministers would be hard put to know what to teach, from their own discipline, to members of the psychological professions even if they were specifically asked and salaried to do so."[20] He goes on to plead that ministers recover their historic identity in order better to serve persons who are doing some real soul searching.

A high priority for some theological teachers and pastoral care professionals will be to study, translate, and make available the texts that are now largely unavailable. Many of the most important of these valued treatises simply cannot be purchased. I know of nowhere that you can buy, even through rare book channels, Bishop Burnet's *A Discourse of the Pastoral Care* (1692), or Sailer's *Pastoral Theologie;*[21] you will find them in only a handful of the best libraries in the country. Some works like Augustine's "The Care to be Taken for the Dead" appear in the Nicene and post-Nicene fathers, but the ailing translation is so jumbled as to be virtually unreadable. The translations of the ante-Nicene fathers and the Nicene and post-Nicene fathers, done prior to the turn of this century, are greatly hampered by stilted Victorian phrases. So we have several strata of problems: inaccessibility, out-of-print volumes, the high cost of rare books, poor translations, and add to this the hesitation of book publishers to risk publishing historical themes that are not self-evidently of wide popular interest. These are the obstacles that have stood in the way for some time in bringing these texts back into availability. The hunger is rising as the nonavailability increases.

The Promise of an Enriched Synthesis Between Old and New

At this point it seems fitting to speak, even if tentatively, of the challenge and promise of the road ahead for Christian pastoral care, assuming a gradually increasing accessibility of the basic texts of the tradition. I am not proposing a reactionary archaism that would rigidly repeat culturally determined prejudices of the past. Nor am I

20. Pruyser, *Minister as Diagnostician,* 39–40.
21. Gilbert Burnet, *A Discourse of the Pastoral Care* (1692; London: Baynes, 1818); Jacob Sailer, *Vorlseungen aus der Pastoraltheologie* (Munich: Lentner, 1788).

proposing a radically new model that would transcend this morass with some brilliant innovation. The task that lies ahead is the development of a postmodern, post-Freudian, neoclassical approach to Christian pastoral care that takes seriously the resources of modernity while also penetrating its illusions and, having found the best of modern psychotherapies still problematic, has turned again to the classical tradition for its bearings, yet without disowning what it has learned from modern clinical experience.

In order to do this we must learn in some fresh new ways the courage to give intelligent resistance to the narcissistic imperialism and hedonistic reductionism that prevail both in the culture and, to a large extent, in the churches. This course I have not yet seen, but nothing is more crucial for us in the pastoral care field than to find its ground and possibility. We can no longer afford ourselves the luxury of allowing contemporary psychotherapies to define for us what pastoral care is. The situation comes very close to being a confessional moment (*in statu confessionis*) for those of us to whom the teaching office of the church is committed, at least in the fields of pastoral theology and pastoral care. We must define for ourselves again what pastoral care is and in what sense pastoral theology is and remains theology, and in order to do that we must be carefully instructed by the tradition out of which that understanding can emerge. Otherwise there can be nothing but continued and expanded confusion about professional identity.

The task is not merely that of giving skeptical, critical resistance to present trends, but also that of giving new energies to a wholesome reconstruction of a pastoral care that is informed by Christian theology, able to provide a credible pastoral theodicy; able to work through difficult cases of conscience; aware of the dialectic of grace and freedom, gospel and law; able to point saliently to the providence of God in the midst of our human alienations; aware of the intrinsic connections between community, healing, and proclamation (koinonia, therapeia, and kerygma); and well-grounded in the classical understanding of the Triune God. The prevailing theological method of recent pastoral care has followed the intuition of pietism in placing its stress largely on personal experience, often to the exclusion of historical experience, reason, Scripture, and tradition. The new efforts in neoclassical pastoral care must work out of a sound, wholesome theological method that neglects neither Scripture, tradition, reason, nor experience in the quest to understand how our response to revelation manifests itself in concrete personal and interpersonal decision.

But really, you ask, what can the classical tradition usefully contribute to modern pastoral counseling? What practical difference might it make if it were trying to preserve and develop the achievements of contemporary clinically oriented pastoral care? Although it is far too early to answer these questions with any certainty, there are some general shifts of direction that to a greater or lesser degree I would expect to occur:

Intercessory prayer would again become an important aspect of pastoral counsel.

The antinomianism of contemporary pastoral care (under the tutelege of hedonic pop psychologies) would be more effectively resisted by a more balanced dialectic of gospel and law.

Marriage counseling would tend to function more within the framework of a traditional Christian doctrine of matrimony rather than essentially as a hedonic cost/benefit calculus.

Empathy training for pastoral counseling would be more deliberately and self-consciously grounded in an incarnational understanding of God's participation in human alienation.

Out of our recent history of exaggerated self-expression, compulsive feeling disclosure, and narcissism, we may be in for a new round of experimentation in askesis, self-discipline, self-denial, and rigorism, which might in turn threaten to become exaggerated in a masochistic direction and thus again need the corrective of a balanced Christian anthropology.

The diminished moral power of the previously prevailing momentum of individualistic autonomy and self-assertiveness may call for a new emphasis in group process upon corporate responsibility, mutual accountability, moral self-examination, and social commitment, an emphasis that would be undergirded by studies in Bible and tradition.

We are ready for a new look at the traditional Protestant pattern of regular pastoral visitation, which could open many doors now closed to most secular therapists.

Pastoral counsel would work harder than it is now working to develop a thorough and meaningful pastoral theodicy that takes fully into account the philosophical and moral objections to classical Christian arguments on the problem of evil and the meaning of suffering, yet with new attentiveness to the deeper pastoral intent of that tradition.

The new synthesis would interweave evangelical witness more deliberately into the process of pastoral conversation rather than disavowing witness or disassociating proclamation from thera-peutic dialogue.

Group experimentation would continue, but be rooted with more awareness of classical Christian understandings of witness, serv-ice, and community.

Older therapeutic approaches such as fasting, dietary control, meditation, and concrete acts of restitution would have new importance.

The now atrophied concept of call to ministry may need to be thoroughly restudied and reconceived as a hinge concept of the pastoral office and of ordination.

Contemporary pastoral theology in dialogue with the classical tradition may learn to speak in a more definite way about the spiritual and moral qualifications for ministry, reflecting the tradition's persistent concern for moral character, humility, zeal, and self-denial.

The arts of spiritual direction that have been developed, nurtured, reexamined, and refined over a dozen centuries of pastoral ex-perience may be due for serious restudy. Efforts could be made to bring these resources back into contemporary pastoral inter-actions that presuppose post-Freudian understandings.

Pastoral care would become less prone to messianic faddism, be-cause it would have built into it a critical apparatus more deeply rooted in the Christian tradition.

A nonsexist, nonchauvinist reinterpretation of ministry, prayer, pas-toral care, and spiritual direction would require a serious critical dialogue with tradition, a dialogue that must be as far-ranging as the radical feminists assert and yet able to incorporate the col-lective wisdom of Christian historical experience. Such critical dialogue is worth risking and far better than a simplistic accom-modation to modern individualistic narcissism or reductive naturalisms.

The term *pastoral counseling* would again be reclaimed as an inte-gral part of the pastoral office, intrinsically correlated with lit-urgy, preaching, and the nurture of Christian community and relatively less identified with purely secularized, nonecclesial, theologically emasculated fee-basis counseling.

The Moment of Truth

Pastoral counseling need not be ashamed of many of its achieve-ments in the twentieth century. But it cannot boast of its biblical grounding, historical awareness, or theological clarity. The European churches are learning rapidly from American pastoral care of our clinical training, supervisory programs, and therapeutic skills, but if we ask how well we have integrated these achievements into ordained ministry, or a clear conception of the pastoral office, the answer must be—"very superficially." At worst, pastoral counseling has learned that it can get along quite well without Christ and the apostles, Scriptures, ancient ecumenical church teaching, and with minimal pastoral reference. At times it amounts to a curious disavowal of professional ministry in the name of professionalism.

I have tried as a theologian to defend fee-basis counseling. In the past I have even sought to provide for it a biblical and theological rationale. But today I find myself hard put to account for the now all-too-familiar pattern of the ordained, full-time, fee-basis pastoral counselor who has no congregation, no explicit pastoral role, and cannot tell you the inner relation between the therapeutic task and the Christian community. One has to skate pretty far out on the thin ice of secular theology in order easily to embrace the premise that this is all there is to the pastoral office—diakonia without marturia, counseling without kerygma—and that pastoral counseling may be fully expressed without any reference to Christian revelation, baptism, Lord's Supper, ministry, ordination, prayer, Scripture, and the language of the religious community out of which the counseling emerges and to which it is presumably accountable.

Protestant and Catholic pastoral counseling has been drawn into a collusive relationship with an accommodationist theology that has seduced it into a partial or substantive disavowal of historic Christianity, its sacraments, doctrine, ordination, and self-giving service. I give you a case in point: with the emergence of government-supported therapies, to our amazement it has now suddenly become a pocketbook question for some fee-basis counselors as to whether they are in any definable sense Christian pastors, and on that answer hangs the fateful possibility of their being able to get on government payrolls as counselors and consultants. The specter of government-sponsored pastoral counseling not only raises grave questions of church and state boundaries; it also raises puzzling questions about the extent of disavowal of religious orientation and witness implicit in tax-supported counseling.

This has unexpectedly placed pastoral counseling at a confessional crossroad (*in statu confessionis*).[22] Some will experience the question

22. Cf. Dietrich Bonhoeffer, *Letters and Papers from Prison*, trans. Reginald Fuller (New York: Macmillan, 1953).

starkly: As a pastoral counselor, will I in good conscience accept income from the government at the cost of disavowing implicitly or explicitly all religious perspective or reference in my counseling process? If I make that disavowal, to what extent can I or the church I serve legitimately regard that as pastoral counseling? What is specifically pastoral about a pastoral counseling that has abandoned the historic pastoral office? Some "professional pastoral counselors" will answer, "Yes, I can in good conscience accept government funding," using as a precedent other ministers who have entered government social services. They will argue that they can fulfill their ministry without word and sacrament, without overt witness or worshiping community, and (why not?) without ordination. Big-brother government involvement in pastoral counseling is only an overt and stark example of what is happening more subtly in fee-basis pastoral counseling generally, with third-party payments on the increase.

What disturbs me most is the fact that such fateful decisions can come so easily and thoughtlessly. For I am aware of the cheap-grace theology that supports them, which I myself to some extent have condoned or at least (until recently) not rejected with determination. That theology has offered pastoral counseling a fleshless Christ, a *logus asarkos*,[23] coupled with a diluted ideology of general ministry that makes no distinction between the ordained ministry and the ministry of the laity, and therefore easily loses track of the specific scriptural entrustment to ordained ministry to secure the apostolic witness through Christian teaching, preaching, and sacramental action.

Just as the Christian martyrs of the second and third centuries were called upon by state power to give assent to the Roman gods, and because they refused entered into a *status confessionis* in which confession of faith was unavoidably required at great cost, so ministry today is coming to such a point where this confession of faith is unavoidable: We will not accept your tax money, surveillance, or support if they require any hint of a disavowal of the God of Abraham, Isaac, and Jacob, and Jesus.

Some will choose one way, some another. But if it is less than a deliberate decision, we deceive ourselves in a deeper way than all the layers of neurotic self-deception that we have learned to analyze. For it is, finally, God with whom we are dealing, who judges justly, and who knows the imaginations of our hearts.

23. See Thomas C. Oden, *Contemporary Theology and Psychotherapy* (Philadelphia: Westminster, 1967), 62–64.

2

Pastoral Care
and the Gospel

LeRoy Aden

Ironically, pastoral care does not have a secure place in the church. Its status and role must be established and clarified, because the church has tended to relate to pastoral care with ambivalence. This ambivalence is seen in seminary curriculums when pastoral care and other functions of ministry are considered secondary to, or mere applications of, the classical disciplines. The ambivalence is also evident in the history of the church.

Martin Luther's ambivalent stance in relation to the cure of souls is an example. On the one hand, it was in regard to an issue concerning the cure of souls that Luther started the Reformation. He was concerned about people who were led to believe that their salvation, or the salvation of a loved one, could be secured by the purchase of letters of indulgence. Throughout his busy career, he retained an active interest in the temporal and eternal welfare of persons. In letters, sermons, commentaries, tracts, in almost everything he said or wrote, Luther's pastoral concern was evident.

On the other hand, Luther manifested a tendency to minimize or even to exclude pastoral care from the mainstream of Christian ministry. In the Augsburg Confession, for example, the task or function of ministry is described as preaching the Word and administering the sacraments. If this statement is understood in a literal sense, pastoral

care is either excluded from the church or confined to the oral proclamation of the Word. In any case, we end up with a truncated ministry that is limited to those occasions when the pastor is dealing with
the Word directly. Preaching becomes the epitome of the office, and
all other functions are judged in its light. Werner Elert crystallizes the
trend: "The office of shepherd *is* the office of preaching. The food for
the sheep is the Gospel, which is offered to them through the ser-
mon. . . . The rule of the shepherd 'consists in feeding, that is, in
preaching; there can be no higher service.' "[1]

Luther is not alone. Saint Paul also manifests an ambiguous stance
toward pastoral care. On the one hand, his encounter with the crucified Christ on the Damascus road made him pastoral. That encounter,
or more precisely his daily assurance of the righteousness of God,
pervaded his whole life and energized his entire ministry, including
his pastoral relationship with troubled persons. On the other hand,
Paul assigns top priority—sometimes even exclusive priority—to proclaiming the Word. He sees himself as an apostle, and as an apostle
he thought he had received a direct commission to preach the gospel
to the Gentiles. He is single-minded about the task, using every occasion to announce the Good News. Other factors reinforce Paul's pen-
chant toward preaching. He believed that proclamation was the sine
qua non of faith, that it was the precondition without which people
could not know or believe in the gospel (Rom. 10:14). In addition, Paul
was dominated by eschatological expectations. He expected the parousia to occur in his generation, maybe in his lifetime, and this expectation inflamed his desire to preach the gospel. "In the limited time
left before the Parousia he [Paul] had to carry the message of Christ
as Lord and Savior of all to the whole Gentile world."[2]

So what is the status and role of pastoral care in the church? Is it
an essential form of Christian ministry, or is it a secondary function
that is important only if it fulfills the primary task of proclaiming the
Word? We will answer that question only as we clarify pastoral care's
relation to the gospel, that is, only as we clarify what pastoral care *is*.
But first it may be helpful to examine the phrase *proclaim the Word*,
that is, to set forth what pastoral care is to *do*.

The Primary Task of Pastoral Care

As we have seen, if "proclaim the Word" is used in a literal sense,
then pastoral care is excluded from the church. It suggests, therefore,

1. Werner Elert, *The Structure of Lutheranism*, trans. W. A. Hansen (Saint Louis:
Concordia, 1962), 366–67.
2. Gunther Bornkamm, *The New Testament: A Guide to Its Writings*, new ed., trans.
Reginald H. and Ilse Fuller (Philadelphia: Fortress, 1973), 75–76.

that the phrase should be understood in a deeper and more inclusive sense. Specifically, this means that the word *proclaim* should not be identified with a particular activity or function (e.g., preaching) but should be understood in a more wholistic sense to refer to the communication of a message or the declaration of an event. Proclaim in this sense can take different forms in ministry, depending on the particular situation involved. More important, proclaim in this sense highlights at least two important theological truths.

First, it is congruent with and an expression of the doctrine of revelation. It expresses that we do not possess the Word but that we must receive it by being told about it. We cannot know God by our own reason or strength, but he must disclose himself to us, which he does supremely in Jesus Christ. It is in this framework that Paul says, "And how are they to believe in him of whom they have never heard?" (Rom. 10:14). Paul would be especially attentive to this truth, for his ministry was to Gentiles who had never heard the gospel. The Word needed to be announced to them. In this kind of situation, proclamation as announcement enjoys an understandable priority.

Second, "proclaim" in a wider sense refers to something deeper than the mere impartation of information. It is not simply talking about an event, not even if it is the Christ event, but it is both a communication of the event and an actualization of it. It delivers or makes real what it is talking about. For example, the proclamation of forgiveness to a repentant individual is an actualization of justification: By God's power the individual *is* forgiven. This is why Paul and others emphasized the announced Word over against the written Word. It is in the sharing of the Word that it becomes what Gerhard O. Forde calls "performative" language, and not just descriptive language. The proclaimed gospel does what it says.

The Word proclaimed, then, becomes the norm and goal of all functions of ministry without necessarily being identified with any one of them. Of course, there is some wisdom in the traditional inclination to identify proclamation with preaching, for preaching is a direct and public attempt to communicate and actualize the Word. In this sense, it is closer to the root meaning of *kerysso* (announce; make known) than other acts of ministry. But in actuality, there is nothing automatic about the connection. Preaching may be a learned discourse, an inspiring or uninspiring flow of words, anything but the effective communication of the gospel. It is proclamation only if it reveals what God is and does for us and makes it operative in the present moment. Besides, Paul implies that to be effective the Word involves more than verbal announcement. It involves exhortation, warning, encouragement, and witness, and "requires unceasing pleading and wooing, with a love that seeks, and is accompanied by a constant care of the individual."[3]

In this larger framework, teaching, caring, and any other act of ministry can be proclamation. As we will see in the case of pastoral care, each function has its own distinctive task to perform in relation to the gospel, but at the same time each one not only can but also should serve the purpose of proclamation. One function cannot replace another, so that where one is the appropriate form of proclamation, it is "for the time being, autonomous, requiring no justification from anything else"[4] or from any other function.

We have now clarified what pastoral care is to *do*, at least in an ultimate sense. How it is to carry out this task will become clearer if we turn to what pastoral care *is*.

The Source of Pastoral Caring

Pastoral care as we know it today is the church's formal expression of our response to the gospel. In other words, we are dealing with an institutionalized activity. While this development may have a certain positive and necessary value, it has had at least two negative effects.

First, it means that pastoral care is seen as the "office and duty" of the pastor instead of being the privilege and responsibility of every Christian. The net effect is to make pastoral care an individual activity that normally occurs between two persons, one of whom is the official representative of the church while the other is an isolated member of it by virtue of his or her special needs. As we will see, this is a far cry from Paul's community-oriented admonition to the Thessalonians: "Therefore encourage one another and build one another up, just as you are doing" (1 Thess. 5:11).

Second, the institutionalization of pastoral care has had a negative effect on the way it is conceived. As Seward Hiltner points out, the term *pastoral* has been used in at least two different ways since the Reformation.[5] On the one hand, it has been used synonymously with the noun *pastor*, which means that whatever pastors do is considered pastoral simply because they do it. The advantage of this formulation is that pastoral is seen as an attitudinal quality. It inheres in pastors and is manifested in everything they do. The disadvantage of this

3. Lothar Coenen, "Proclamation, Preach, Kerygma," in *The New International Dictionary of New Testament Theology*, ed. Colin Brown (Grand Rapids: Zondervan, 1978), 3:54.

4. Seward Hiltner, *Christian Shepherd* (Nashville: Abingdon, 1959), 17.

5. Seward Hiltner, *Preface to Pastoral Theology* (Nashville: Abingdon, 1958), 15–20.

formulation is that the word *pastoral* describes everything in general and therefore nothing in particular. If it refers to everything the pastor does, it loses its distinctiveness and fails to highlight specific acts of care or concern.

On the other hand, the term *pastoral* has been used to refer to a particular function of ministry, primarily the function of caring for individuals and groups within the church. It is not an attitude but an activity, distinguished from the pastor's other activities (e.g., preaching, teaching, and evangelizing). The advantage of this formulation is that it recognizes that there are a variety of functions required of pastors and that their pastoral function is not dominant in everything they do. The disadvantage is that it creates isolated compartments of activity and therefore implies that the pastor goes from one activity to another with no relation between them.

Hiltner attempts to retain the advantage of both formulations while avoiding their weaknesses by suggesting that the term *pastoral* should designate a perspective, not an officeholder or a function. Pastoral, then, becomes an inner stance alongside other possible stances. Specifically, it is a stance of "tender and solicitous concern" that becomes dominant in the pastor's activity when the parishioner's situation makes it relevant. Hiltner's formulation gives him the best of both worlds. It allows him to see pastoral care as an attitude of loving concern that can become active in whatever the pastor is doing. At the same time, it allows him to recognize that there are occasions in ministry when some function besides pastoral care is dominant and determinative.

As a conceptual scheme, Hiltner's formulation is a sophisticated and heuristic approach to pastoral care. It gives us the same advantage it gives him, making pastoral care a specific and fluid disposition of solicitous concern that is responsive to the immediate situation. In spite of this advantage, Hiltner's formulation is not exhaustive. It locates the roots of pastoral care in "the gospel command to heal" but does not go underneath the command to uncover the root experience out of which pastoral care comes. Thus it fails to clarify the essential theological nature of pastoral care. What we need to do is to get beyond the church's institutionalization of pastoral care and to recover the fact that pastoral care is basically a response to the gospel. In a word, this means that pastoral care comes out of faith, when faith is conceived as obedience in love to the neighbor in need. Saint Paul helps us to clarify the point.

For Paul, faith is not intellectual assent or partial trust but a complete openness and giving of oneself to Christ. It puts one's whole being at God's disposal, so much so that Paul can speak of the believer "being in Christ" and Christ "being in him," not in the sense of a mystical union that spells the loss of personal identity but in the sense of surrendering completely to Christ and being bound over to his service. For Paul, then, faith is primarily obedience, where obedience is not a legalistic response to laws but a total and unconditional belonging to Christ. It is a new life in which I live, yet not I but Christ who lives in me.

For Paul, life in Christ is life given over to the neighbor in need. Faith understood as obedience expresses itself in love, not a "spiritual" love that stays with God but a love that manifests itself concretely in relation to the neighbor. Paul is constant on this point. For him, love of the neighbor is not simply a characteristic of the new life but its whole content and mode. "Owe no one anything, except to love one another; for he who loves his neighbor has fulfilled the law" (Rom. 13:8). "So faith, hope, love abide, these three; but the greatest of these is love" (1 Cor. 13:13). "And above all these put on love, which binds everything together in perfect harmony" (Col. 3:14).[6]

Paul is talking about a radical change in human relationships. He is talking about love that takes the form of servanthood. In Greek thought as in New Testament thought, the basic meaning of servanthood is to serve or to wait at table. For the Greeks, this menial task, even if conducted voluntarily, represented a humiliating and undesirable status. Intent on the perfect development of their own personality, they put top priority on ruling and being served. Paul follows Christ who, while he did not deny the commonly accepted impression that the one who is served is greater than the one who serves, nevertheless declared that the Son of man came to serve and not to be served. At the same time, he expands the meaning of service beyond its original context. It now includes many activities—from giving food, shelter, or clothes to visiting the sick and imprisoned. Thus it is a comprehensive term referring to any loving assistance that can be rendered to the neighbor.

Paul maintains that the Christian is to serve the neighbor at a point of specific need. Paul believes that the neighbor's greatest need is to be loved, but he also recognizes other needs that deserve love's consideration. Those who are weak in the faith are to be supported by those who are strong. Those who are burdened are to be helped "in a spirit of gentleness." Those who are hungry are to be fed; and those who weep should receive understanding. Paul nowhere presents an exhaustive list of personal and interpersonal needs. In fact, he is usually more concerned about needs that relate to the whole community, but by clarifying our responsibility to the needy neighbor he has given

6. See also Galatians 5:6 and Romans 13:9.

us the prototype of all pastoral care. *Pastoral care is a response of love and service to the neighbor in need in response to what God is and does for us.* In a word, it is faith taking the form of servant.

Paul provides us with a new and heuristic metaphor for pastoral care. Pastoral theologians, past and present, have used the image of a shepherd to describe the person who cares. For example, the image is central in Hiltner's thought, even though he is aware of its short-comings. While the image of a shepherd has been and will continue to be useful, it is not radical enough to exhaust the nature and purpose of pastoral ministry. It highlights the idea of patient, loving, and responsible action, but it does not give expression to the paradoxical and salvific truth out of which pastoral care comes. On the contrary, Paul never lets us forget that God accepts in spite of our being unacceptable, that he loves and forgives even though we continue to show enmity and disbelief toward him. Out of this unconditional, undeserved acceptance flows a love that seeks to serve even as it has been served.

Paul reinforces the point when, contrary to all biblical witness before him, he puts affliction and comfort in paradoxical relation to each other. Apparently in Asia he and Timothy were "so utterly, unbearably crushed that we despaired of life itself" (2 Cor. 1:8). When Paul mentions the incident to the Corinthians, he quickly adds that he and Timothy were comforted by the "God of all comfort," that they came to know God not only as a "Father of mercies" but also as a God of encouragement and consolation. And how are they to respond to this blessing? To what end were they comforted? "So that we may be able to comfort those who are in any affliction, with the comfort with which we ourselves are comforted by God" (2 Cor. 1:4). In other words, they are to respond to God's comfort by giving comfort to others.

For Paul, nothing less than the metaphor of servant or, more precisely, of slave, will do. Like the metaphor of shepherd, sevant expresses solicitous attention to needy persons and a caring attempt to meet their needs. But servant goes beyond this. Unlike shepherd, it connotes status to the one who is served, and not to the one who serves. Actually, it takes the focus away from the issue of status and places it on the task to be done. Not the personality or position of the one who serves but only the fact that there is a service to be rendered to someone in need, is important.

Furthermore, in terms of knowledge the servant metaphor implies that the server needs to be an expert only in the art of serving. It is the one who is served who determines need and whether or not that need has been properly met. And in terms of need itself, the servant metaphor allows for a great variety of need and therefore a great many ways in which one can serve—from the giving of care to the giving of clothes, from the need to hold to the need to call into account.

In spite of the advantages of the servant metaphor, I do not anticipate a ground swell for servant over shepherd as a basic metaphor for pastoral care. Fortunately, I have no great vested interest in the term. My primary concern is that we are clear about the root experience out of which Christian pastoral care comes. Our caring is a result of our having been cared for, and not vice versa. It is a product of what we have received, and not of what we possess. In other words, pastoral care is not a prejustification activity that derives from our own loving nature but a postjustification activity that expresses our joy and appreciation for what we have been given. It exists only after we have experienced and have been transformed by God's grace and forgiveness. Any care before that moment is not really pastoral care but work righteousness—an attempt to earn God's forgiveness by meritorious deeds of love and service. In this sense, pastoral care says little about the servant who cares and much about the Master whose love is concretized. It witnesses to the power of God that is at work in and through persons to provide care for those in need. It proclaims God's love, not necessarily by words but by gracious acts of service.

Conclusion

Clarification of what pastoral care *is* has identified how pastoral care is to carry out its primary task of proclaiming the Word. Above all, it is not to throw the gospel at the situation nor is it to preach the Word to persons after the pastor has heard their story. Instead it is to relate the Word to specific need, to embody it in a living relationship of loving service in a way that is appropriate to the situation. In this sense, it is a very human act, person ministering to person, even though it flows out of what God is and does for us rather than out of our own inner resources.

Finally, we need to return to our original question: Is pastoral care an essential or a secondary dimension of Christian ministry? If pastoral care is indeed our response of love and service to what God is and does for us, it is an essential form of proclamation which, under certain circumstances, takes precedence over every other form of ministry. Its precedence is established by its ability to disclose and make real God's love and healing in an efficacious way. That is the basic task of pastoral care, and in certain situations that task can not be performed by any other form of proclamation, that is, by any other function of Christian ministry.

3

The Bible's Role in Pastoral Care and Counseling:
Four Basic Principles

DONALD CAPPS

Among persons involved in seminary and clinical pastoral education, there is growing consensus that pastoral care needs to be more deeply rooted in the Christian tradition. They sense that pastoral care has been too enamored of psychological and psychotherapeutic theories, and insufficiently grounded in the theology and piety of the Christian faith. Various proposals are being made for the recovery of our Christian roots. Thomas C. Oden has demonstrated the value of the ancient patristic tradition for modern pastoral care.[1] The recent publication of a number of books on the Bible's role in pastoral care and counseling is another clear indication of our concern to rediscover our Christian roots.[2] To me, the biblical approach is especially

1. Thomas C. Oden, *Pastoral Theology: Essentials of Ministry* (San Francisco: Harper and Row, 1983).
2. Jay E. Adams, *Competent to Counsel* (Nutley, N.J.: Presbyterian and Reformed, 1970); idem, *The Use of the Scriptures in Counseling* (Grand Rapids: Baker, 1975); William B. Oglesby, Jr., *Biblical Themes for Pastoral Care* (Nashville: Abingdon, 1980); Eugene Petersen, *Five Smooth Stones for Pastoral Work* (Atlanta: John Knox, 1980); Donald Capps, *Biblical Approaches to Pastoral Counseling* (Philadelphia: Westminster, 1981).

41

promising because the Christian faith is founded in the Bible. More-over, since Vatican II, the call for renewed attention to the Bible's role in pastoral care no longer serves an exclusively Protestant agenda. This is important, because a major achievement of the pastoral care field in recent years has been its broadening ecumenicity.

In this chapter, I will first review the recent history of the Bible's role in pastoral care and counseling. Then I will identify the basic principles that have emerged during this period for how the Bible is to be used in pastoral care and counseling. We have made considerable progress over the past five decades toward clarifying the Bible's role in pastoral care and counseling. But these gains have so far gone un-detected because we have not taken the trouble to identify them in any systematic fashion. I suggest that, by this time, we have reached general consensus on two principles, are continuing to struggle over a third, and are just now in the process of elaborating a fourth. To make this argument, I will take a historical view of the Bible's role in pastoral care and counseling, focusing on the period from the mid-1930s to the mid-1980s.

Historical Review

In developing my own approach to the Bible's role in pastoral care and counseling. I made a rather extensive review of the literature from 1930 to the present.[3] The 1930 date was somewhat arbitrary, since the Bible has played an important role in pastoral care throughout the centuries. But the 1930s mark the emergence of the "modern" pastoral care movement, whose hallmarks are its appropriation of contempo-rary psychological theories and methods, its commitment to clinical pastoral education, and its emphasis on the pastor as practical theo-logian and personal counselor. In reviewing the literature, I wanted to find out how the Bible's role in pastoral care has been understood in recent times. Was it supplanted by psychological theories? Was its use downplayed or even discouraged, as is commonly alleged? Were pos-itive proposals made for its use in pastoral care situations? Were any principles formulated to guide ministers in their pastoral use of the Bible?

Through this literature review, I found that there are basically four identifiable periods in the modern pastoral care movement's approach to the Bible.

3. Donald Capps, *Life Cycle Theory and Pastoral Care* (Philadelphia: Fortress, 1983).

Emerging Consensus

The emerging consensus period (1936–1960) began with the publication of Richard C. Cabot and Russell L. Dicks's enormously influential book, *The Art of Ministering to the Sick,* and continued into the late 1940s and 1950s with Seward Hiltner's chapter on "religious resources" in *Pastoral Counseling,* Wayne E. Oates's *The Bible in Pastoral Care,* and Carroll A. Wise's *Psychiatry and the Bible.*[4] During this period, general agreement was reached about the Bible's major uses in pastoral care and counseling. The Bible was seen as a "religious resource" that could offer comfort and moral guidance. It could also aid exploration of the counselee's inner dynamics. Some called it a diagnostic instrument that, in the hands of a skilled pastor, could reveal much about a person's inner conflicts and emotional distress.

However, during this period the Bible was not viewed as the basis for establishing the overall objectives of pastoral care and counseling. For this, theology was the major resource, with primary emphasis on theological understandings of the human condition and the Christian faith's response to that condition.[5] It was generally assumed that these theological understandings were consistent with biblical tradition, but this assumption was not always subjected to careful scrutiny. In general, there was more concern to establish the compatibility between theology and the psychological theories that were gaining widespread acceptance among the educated clergy. Of course, this is not to say that the major writers during this period were nonbiblical in their orientation to pastoral care and counseling. The literature published during this period provides substantial evidence that the authors were steeped in the Bible, and had a deep personal attachment to it. Yet, the Bible was viewed mainly as a "religious resource" for pastoral care and counseling. Biblical perspectives only indirectly informed care and counseling goals. The Bible was certainly used, but its use was essentially ad hoc. Especially in the counseling setting, the pastor was free to use it or not. As a resource, its use was dependent mainly on the counselee's situation and the pastor's personal comfort or discomfort with its use. Serious attention was never given to the possibility that the Bible might actually set the goals of counseling and inform its processes. I will return to this criticism of the emerging

4. Richard C. Cabot and Russell L. Dicks, *The Art of Ministering to the Sick* (New York: Macmillan, 1936); Seward Hiltner, *Pastoral Counseling* (Nashville: Abingdon, 1949); Wayne E. Oates, *The Bible in Pastoral Care* (Philadelphia: Westminster, 1953); Carroll A. Wise, *Psychiatry and the Bible* (New York: Harper and Row, 1956).

5. Daniel Day Williams, *The Minister and the Care of Souls* (New York: Harper and Row, 1961).

consensus school later, when I discuss the principles already alluded to.

European Interlude

During the European interlude period (1960–1970), there were no significant new developments in America on the Bible's role in pastoral care and counseling. General consensus that the Bible can be a valuable religious resource continued throughout the 1960s. However, European pastoral theologians, particularly Eduard Thurneysen with his *Theology of Pastoral Care*,[6] addressed the issue from a new standpoint. Rather than viewing the Bible as a valuable religious resource, Thurneysen began with the Word of God, and suggested that pastoral counseling is a conversation that proceeds from the Word of God and leads to the Word of God. In this essentially Barthian approach to pastoral counseling, Thurneysen was careful not simply to equate the Word of God with the Bible as such. The language of the Bible does not make it the Word of God. Rather, the Bible *becomes* the living Word of God when it is the vehicle for conviction of sin and assurance of forgiveness.

Through emphasis on the Word of God, Thurneysen gave the Bible a very different status from what it had during the emerging consensus period. He agreed that the Bible need not be directly quoted in the pastoral visit or counseling session, but he stressed that the Bible itself provides paradigms of pastoral conversations in which there is conviction of sin and assurance of forgiveness. The stories of the prophet Nathan and David (2 Sam. 11) and Jesus and the Samaritan woman at Jacob's well (John 4) are cases in point. Thus, the Bible is not primarily viewed as a resource for comforting, guiding, and diagnosing the counselee. Instead, it models effective confrontation with the Word of God leading to conviction of sin and assurance of forgiveness. For Thurneysen, the whole purpose of pastoral care and counseling is to bring the counselee to an awareness of sin and appropriation of God's forgiving mercy and love. With this theologically informed understanding of the objectives of pastoral care and counseling, the Bible becomes much more central to the whole process. Given its powerful association with the Word of God, the Bible has a central role in the care and counseling process.

Conservative Developments

In some respects, the European interlude period set the stage for the third phase. The conservative developments period began around

6. Eduard Thurneysen, *A Theology of Pastoral Care*, trans. Jack A. Worthington and Thomas Wieser (Atlanta: John Knox, 1962).

1970 and has continued to the present. This phase was initiated through Jay E. Adams's *Competent to Counsel* and Gary R. Collins's *Effective Counseling*. Adams's subsequent book, *The Use of the Scriptures in Counseling*, has also been influential.[7] In Adams's approach to the Bible's role in Christian counseling, the emerging consensus period's effort to reconcile theological concepts and psychological theories is rejected. In fact, modern psychological theories are vigorously and totally rejected. The Scriptures are the sole guide for both counselor and counselee. Nor does Adams retain Thurneysen's distinction between the Word of God and the biblical form in which the Word is communicated. Thus, he does not share Thurneysen's view that biblical texts need not always be referred to in the pastoral conversation. However, he does share Thurneysen's view that the purpose of pastoral counseling is to bring the counselee to a conviction of sin and assurance of forgiveness, though, here again, there are not-so-subtle differences in how he articulates this. On the one hand, his view of sin is more narrowly defined. Both say that sin is ultimately offense against God, but Adams defines this offense almost exclusively in terms of rebellion, or a flaunting of God's directives. No doubt this heavy emphasis on sin as rebellion has partly to do with his counseling focus. Many of his cases concern parent-child conflicts for which he advocates strong disciplinary measures. These children and adolescents are rebelling against parental and societal controls, or against a situation of normlessness where such controls are absent. Also, unlike Thurneysen, Adams links biblical texts that assure forgiveness with texts that stress the importance of holy living. Adams will never be accused of offering cheap grace.

Adams's critics point out that he deals with biblical texts in atomistic fashion. Thurneysen believes the Bible has a unifying theme of conviction of sin and assurance of forgiveness, and all biblical texts are to be viewed in the light of this theme that, for him, is the very gospel itself. Adams does not deny that the Bible has some thematic unity, but it does not stand out either in his biblical exegesis or in his counseling approach. He treats the Bible more atomistically, virtually as a vast collection of individual verses. He seems especially fond of the biblical text that is legitimately viewed this way, namely, Proverbs, but it is almost as though he uses Proverbs to establish his exegetical method for the Bible as a whole. In any event, biblical verses and phrases are chosen for their relevance to the counselee's situation. Relevance is determined not on the basis of topical similarity, but on

7. Adams, *Competent to Counsel*; Gary R. Collins, *Effective Counseling* (Carol Stream, Ill.: Creation House, 1972); Adams, *Use of the Scriptures*.

the telos or purpose of the text. This means that the counselor must understand the purpose or telos of biblical texts, here mainly understood as individual verses and phrases. Some verses are overt as to their telos: "These things are written so that you may believe," while the telos of other verses needs to be discerned. On the basis of 2 Timothy 3, we can anticipate that the telos of a biblical verse will be to either teach, convict, correct, or train in righteousness.

The major contribution of the conservative developments period is that is has raised questions about the adequacy of the emerging consensus view that the Bible is a "religious resource" for pastoral care and counseling. Does not this effectively relegate the Bible to secondary status? Ought not the Bible have a major, perhaps the central, role in setting the agenda for pastoral care and counseling? The emerging consensus period affirmed, of course, that it is the role of theology to set the goals of pastoral care and counseling, but, as conservatives were pointing out, psychotherapeutic theories and methods were receiving considerably more attention than the theologies whose purpose was to determine the legitimacy of these theories and methods in Christian counseling. The unintended yet very real result was that the goals of pastoral care and counseling were being set by these theories and methods, and thus appeared not to differ significantly from the goals of psychotherapy itself. Few conservatives agreed with Adams that the solution would be a thoroughgoing rejection of all psychotherapeutic theories and methods. Indeed, many took the view that certain psychological and psychotherapeutic theories actually support conservative theological positions. These conservatives are now engaged in the very project that engaged many representatives of the emerging consensus period, which is to explore the relationships between theology and contemporary psychology.[8]

Moderate Resurgence

This brings us to the fourth phase in the modern pastoral care movement's approach to the Bible, the moderate resurgence period, which dates from about 1975 and, as the third period, continues into the present. This phase was signaled in John B. Cobb, Jr.'s, *Theology and Pastoral Care*, where he called for a certain pastoral bilingualism, with pastors able to reflect on parishioner's problems in biblical as well as contemporary language.[9] It began to flourish with David K. Switzer's

8. John D. Carter and Bruce Narramore, *The Integration of Psychology and Theology: An Introduction* (Grand Rapids: Zondervan, 1979); Gary R. Collins, *Psychology and Theology: Prospects for Integration*, ed. H. Newton Malony (Nashville: Abingdon, 1981).

9. John B. Cobb, Jr., *Theology and Pastoral Care* (Philadelphia: Fortress, 1977).

Pastor, Preacher, Person, which addresses the pastoral care approach to controversial biblical texts on divorce and husband-wife relationships.[10] However, evidence that moderates were now serious about the Bible's role in care and counseling did not really appear until the early 1980s, when three books focused on this issue appeared.[11] This moderate resurgence continues with the more recent publication of Wilhelm H. Wuellner and Robert C. Leslie's *The Surprising Gospel* and two books on hermeneutics and pastoral care.[12] Cedric B. Johnson's book indicates that conservatives are also vitally interested in biblical hermeneutics and its implications for pastoral care.[13]

Like the conservatives, these moderates have significant differences among themselves, but they have in common the view that the Bible is more than a resource for pastoral care and counseling. For them, the Bible has a major contribution to make to the very process and goals of pastoral care and counseling. Moderates writing today give the Bible a more central role in pastoral counseling than did their predecessors in the latter decades of the emerging consensus period. They envision the Bible having a more influential role in shaping the counseling process and establishing its ultimate objectives. Like conservatives, however, they do not all agree on how the Bible's role in this regard is to be understood. For example, William B. Oglesby, Jr., contends that the Bible contains a unifying theme, namely, how God is acting for and with humankind toward reconciliation and restoration. Like Adams, he emphasizes that sin is the fundamental human condition to which this central biblical theme is addressed. However, unlike Adams, Oglesby does not see rebellion as the essential characteristic of sin. For him, sin is a denial of one's essential nature as a "creature with creativity." By being less or claiming more than this, one's relationship to God—the Creator—is undermined. Thus the effect of sin is broken relationship and salvation is the restoration of relationship. Oglesby then proposes that the Bible elaborates various subthemes relating to this basic unifying theme, including initiative

10. David K. Switzer, *Pastor, Preacher, Person: Developing a Pastoral Ministry in Depth* (Nashville: Abingdon, 1979).

11. Oglesby, *Biblical Themes for Pastoral Care;* Petersen, *Five Smooth Stones;* Capps, *Biblical Approaches to Pastoral Counseling.*

12. Wilhelm H. Wuellner and Robert C. Leslie, *The Surprising Gospel* (Nashville: Abingdon, 1984); Charles V. Gerkin, *The Living Human Document* (Nashville: Abingdon, 1983); Donald Capps, *Pastoral Care and Hermeneutics* (Philadelphia: Fortress, 1984).

13. Cedric B. Johnson, *The Psychology of Biblical Interpretation* (Grand Rapids: Zondervan, 1983).

and freedom, fear and faith, conformity and rebellion, death and re-
birth, risk and redemption.

Because the breaking and restoration of relationship is the Bible's
central theme, Oglesby is especially partial to those psychotherapeutic
theories that give primacy to the counselor-counselee relationship. For
him, this means client-centered and Gestalt therapy. Other types of
psychotherapy, which he calls knowing and behavior therapies, are
not dismissed, since the Bible also takes seriously the role of insight
and behavioral change in the sin-salvation dynamic, but the restoration of relationship, and the therapies that focus on relationship as the
primary means of change, are fundamental. The goal of pastoral care
and counseling is therefore to contribute, in concert with God's own
initiatives, toward the reconciliation and restoration of human
relationships.

In contrast to Oglesby, Eugene Peterson and Donald Capps do not
focus on the thematic unity of the Bible, but on its literary forms. For
example, Peterson centers on the Megilloth, or the five biblical texts
that are assigned readings at five of Israel's annual acts of worship.
These include Song of Songs, Ruth, Lamentations, Ecclesiastes, and
Esther. Capps focuses on the form of the lament (found in Psalms,
certain prophetic literature, and the Gospels), the proverbs, and the
parable. He identifies the underlying theological structure of each of
these forms, and claims that once the form is theologically understood,
it can inform the goals of pastoral care and counseling. Unlike Oglesby,
whose view that the Bible has a unified theme leads to a unitary view
of pastoral care and counseling as well, each biblical form for Capps
entails different pastoral care and counseling goals. The lament form
relates to pastoral care of the bereaved, in which the goal is to comfort;
the proverb form relates to premarital counseling, whose goal is to
provide moral guidance; and the parable relates best to marriage and
family counseling because the parable is concerned with broken, distorted, or otherwise troubled relationships. Here the goal is the re-
structuring of the counselee's perceptions of self, world, and others,
including God, who is the eternal Other. In this view, the Bible provides a less integrated conception of what pastoral care and counseling
are all about than Oglesby's perspective, but it conveys a less atomistic
view than Adams's approach to biblical texts.

Those authors who center on the Bible's literary forms are guided
by an important theological consideration. To them, a given literary
form makes possible certain kinds of divine revelations or disclosures
and precludes others. In an important essay entitled "Toward a Hermeneutic of the Idea of Revelation," Paul Ricoeur focuses on five literary forms of the Bible: prophetic, narrative, prescriptive, wisdom,

hymnic; and proposes that each is revelatory, but in different ways.[14] The narrative or story form always points back to a founding event in which God was originally revealed, such as the exodus or Christ's passion. The hymnic form is revelatory through its formation of emotions that transcend the everyday situations that inspire them; thence, a psalm of lament is applicable to bereavement, whether or not this was the original situation that led to its being written. Each literary form is potentially revelatory in its own unique way. Each discloses God to us, but in its own singular manner.

Because the Bible consists of a great variety of literary forms, it is difficult to think of the Bible as having an essential unity. Of course, it might be argued that, by emphasizing the disclosive capacities of literary forms, these authors indirectly introduce a unitary theme, namely, that the Bible is fundamentally concerned with humans' experience of God's self-disclosure. If so, Oglesby's theme of reconciliation and restoration of relationships would be one of various subthemes describing God's self-disclosure. It would not be the only theme, for the apocalyptic literature of the Bible discloses a God of judgment and wrath, of ultimate irreconciliation. Moreover, literary forms such as the proverbs and the pastoral epistle disclose a God who is vitally concerned with moral formation, sanctified living, and growth toward holiness. By emphasizing reconciliation and restoration of relationship, Oglesby does not give as much attention to biblical themes of sanctification. The two biblical emphases that he considers subordinate to relationship, knowing and behaving, are typically invoked by those who believe that growth in wisdom and holiness are evidence of God's self-disclosure to us.

By centering on literary forms in the Bible, both Capps and Peterson suggest that the structure of a biblical form may directly inform the pastoral care and counseling process. For Capps, the structure of the lament, with its elements of address to God, complaint, confession of trust, petition, words of assurance, and vow to praise God, can be used to inform the grief counseling process, giving intentional shape to this process. Peterson makes similar use of the structure of the Book of Lamentations, which employs an acrostic device in repetitive fashion. Peterson applies this structural device to pastoral care of the bereaved, arguing that we should not view the grief process as a series of stages only, but as a cyclical process that is repeated over and over again. These two examples suggest that disclosure of God is not only in the Bible's content but also in its form, and change is effected through the

14. Paul Ricoeur, "Toward a Hermeneutic of the Idea of Revelation," in *Essays on Biblical Interpretation*, ed. Lewis C. Mudge (Philadelphia: Westminster, 1980), 73–118.

intentional use of biblical forms. The forms guide the care and counseling process, and establish its goals. The bereaved are caringly guided
through the stages of the lament. Although there is considerable vari-
ation in individuals' movement through the stages, and, as Peterson
suggests, some repetition of the stages, the ultimate goal is known to
the pastor from the very beginning. This goal is to enable the grieving
to come to that point, eventually, where they can vow to praise God
in spite of, or even because of, their experience of loss.

Four Basic Principles

My purpose in identifying these four historical stages is not to praise
one or another phase and castigate others. Obviously, I consider myself
to be in the moderate resurgence group. But I believe we should put
aside our partisan blinders and take an unbiased view of what each
of these phases has contributed to our understanding of the Bible's
role in pastoral care and counseling. I suggest that four basic principles have emerged from this fifty-year history. Two of these principles
were established in the early decades of the emerging consensus period. The third was established in the later decades of the emerging
consensus and it has been challenged and/or modified by the three
subsequent periods. The fourth principle has roots in the European
interlude period, but it has been most clearly articulated in the conservative development and moderate resurgence periods. Since this
fourth principle has emerged during my own involvement in the issue,
my way of articulating it reflects my own orientation within the moderate perspective. Conservatives would probably articulate it differently, and I invite them to do so. In fact, I believe that Adams has
offered a version of it in his chapter on the Holy Spirit in *Competent
to Counsel*. I would emphasize that there were those in the emerging
consensus period, such as Oates, who in my judgment would intui-
tively accept this fourth principle. My point is not that it was openly
rejected during the emerging consensus period, but that it was never
explicitly formulated. What was formulated is the valuable but ultimately limited view of the Bible as a religious resource for pastoral
care and counseling. Finally, I will be noting that this fourth principle
has led to proposals that the third principle be substantially modified
to bring it into conformity to the fourth. I myself support modification
of the third principle if the rationale for this is the fourth principle
itself and not a gratuitous attack on psychological and psychotherapeutic theories. Let us now take a careful look at the four principles.

1. *The principle of relevance.* This principle says that whatever use
is made of the Bible in pastoral care and counseling, this use should

be guided by the particular needs and circumstances of the person being helped. The key issue here is the relevance of the text to the situation. Books and articles written during the emerging consensus period often admonished pastors to choose their texts carefully to insure that the text fits the parishioner's situation or problem. Certain texts are appropriate for the grieving, other texts fit the birth of a child, still others are helpful for persons facing a difficult life-decision, and so forth. Much of the impetus behind the pastoral care movement at the outset was the desire for more effective pastoral care of the sick. Therefore, this principle of relevance was especially directed toward pastors engaged in hospital visitation. In the hospital setting, a well-chosen text can have a tremendous effect on the morale of the ill person, and on the family members who are present in the room. A poorly chosen text is likely to have no effect or evoke a negative re-action. As the pastoral care movement became increasingly oriented toward pastoral counseling in the 1950s and 1960s, the principle of relevance still obtained. Pastors engaged in pastoral counseling were similarly advised to choose biblical texts carefully and judiciously. Often, they were warned against any quoting of the Bible that would distract the counseling process from the problem at hand.[15]

2. *The principle of sensitivity.* This principle says that the use of the Bible should reflect pastoral sensitivity to the individual's physical, psychological, or spiritual limitations. Whereas the previous principle emphasizes the text's appropriateness for the situation, this principle stresses its fittingness for a given individual. A certain biblical text may be appropriate to the situation of bereavement, but inappropriate for this grieving person at this time. One criticism I often hear from readers of Adams's *Use of the Scriptures in Counseling* is that he chooses texts for their relevance to the situation but without sufficient sensitivity to the peculiar cicumstances of the individual. This insensitivity is perhaps based on principle. To the counselee who says, "My situation is so different," he responds with 1 Corinthians 10:13: "No temptation has overtaken you that is not common to man."[16] Yet this text applies to temptation, not the uniquely personal way in which individuals experience universal problems. In addition, this tendency toward insensitivity is exacerbated by the fact that Adams, much like Thurneysen, operates on the assumption that whoever comes in for counseling is a sinner. His case of Laurie is an example of this.[17] She is charged with sinfulness while her husband, who happened not to

15. Hiltner, *Pastoral Counseling*, 208–9.
16. Adams, *Use of the Scriptures*, 81.
17. Ibid., 81–83.

come for counseling, goes unscathed. This assumption precludes offering counselees assurance that in this instance they are not at fault, a crucial point in cases involving rape and other forms of physical and psychological abuse where the victim is often charged with provoking the assault. And, of course, this assumption is irrelevant to those counseling situations, often encountered in bereavement or premarital counseling, where personal fault is not at issue.

During the emerging consensus period, much attention was paid to the counselee's spiritual limitations, especially inability to respond to the offered text in the manner intended by the pastor. The counselee's lack of biblical knowledge was noted as a problem in this regard.[18] The counselee may harbor resentment or hostility toward the Bible for what it may symbolize; for example, an unhappy childhood attributable in part to cruelty inflicted by intensely religious parents. Switzer also deals with the opposite problem (i.e. the counselee's misunderstanding of a biblical text becoming a barrier to a resolution of the problem in a mature Christian manner).[19] The general rule of thumb advocated during the emerging consensus period was that the pastor ought not to make a biblical reference if there was the possibility that the counselee would misinterpret the pastor's intentions or the meaning of the text. No doubt this good advice has nonetheless provided some pastors a means of rationalizing their reluctance to allow the Bible to inform their counseling. Moreover, as Paul W. Pruyser has pointed out in *The Minister as Diagnostician*, most persons come to the pastor with their problem because they have diagnosed it as being in some sense a spiritual problem.[20] They may have marital problems or problems in their work, but they sense that these problems have deeper spiritual roots. Thus they have expectations of having their problem discussed in religious terms, and this often means biblical references and allusions.

3. *The principle of consistency.* This principle says that whatever use is made of the Bible in pastoral care and counseling, this use should be consistent with the counseling principles and methods that inform the whole process. It addresses the very real concern that the pastor's introduction of biblical references into the counseling process may actually impede or frustrate the pastor's own goals. In such cases, it is better for the pastor to restrain the impulse to make biblical allusions and instead continue to focus on the counselee's own situation. This principle was established during the emerging consensus

18. Hiltner, *Pastoral Counseling*, 203.
19. Switzer, *Pastor, Preacher, Person*.
20. Paul W. Pruyser, *The Minister as Diagnostician* (Philadelphia: Westminster, 1976).

period, but in its later stages, when the focus of the movement had shifted somewhat from the hospital to the counseling room. It supported the view that the Bible may be a valuable religious resource, if its use is consistent with the goals that already inform the counseling process. As we have seen, these goals were to be arrived at on theological grounds, but it was often the case during the 1950s and 1960s that the goals were actually determined by psychotherapeutic theories. Thus, a principle that would be acceptable to most of us if the counseling principles were arrived at theologically, looks much more dubious when they are explicit or implicitly set by psychotherapeutic theories. In this case, the principle of consistency relegates the Bible to secondary status, but in a more fundamental way, silences the biblical voice. Could it not be the case that the Bible works at cross-purposes with the counseling principles and methods because they are incompatible with the Christian faith? As we have seen, this question was raised during the conservative developments period, though it should also be noted that it was raised during the 1960s by various moderates who were troubled by the attention given to psychotherapeutic theories at the expense of theological and biblical conceptions.

I will suggest a modified version of this principle of consistency based on the fourth principle. But first, I would draw attention to the fact that the first two principles have to do with the person receiving pastoral care, while the third principle concerns the actual goals and methods of the care and counseling process itself. We should not be surprised, therefore, that this principle has evoked considerable disagreement.

4. *The principle of the Bible as a change agent.* This principle says that whatever use is made of the Bible in pastoral care and counseling, it should be informed by the counselor's awareness that biblical texts have the power to change attitudes, behavior, and perceptions. How is this possible? How is the Bible able to be a change agent? In *The Art of Pastoral Conversation*, Gaylord Noyce says that the Bible is like a voice from outside; it has an "otherness" or "alien quality" about it.[21] Thus, it effects change because it shakes us out of our usual approach to life's problems, challenging us to take a perspective on our problems that we have not yet considered taking. As might be expected, I attribute the Bible's "alien quality," and thus its capacity to change lives, to its disclosive power. The Bible is a change agent because it discloses a world in which God is actively engaged. This disclosure challenges us to perceive our situation in terms not only of

21. Gaylord Noyce, *The Art of Pastoral Conversation* (Atlanta: John Knox, 1981), 117–23.

what *is* happening, humanly speaking, but also of what *may be* happening: divine activity. In this way, a biblical text that is disclosive opens to the parishioner a new way of being-in-the-world. This change in life can be manifest in various ways: attitudinal change, behavioral change, and so forth; but what is almost invariably involved is change in perception. One sees life differently when one sees it from the perspective of God's real presence in the world. Psychological and psychotherapeutic theories that deal with perceptual reorientation are especially valuable for describing the change that is brought about when the disclosure of God is appropriated by the individual.[22]

This principle also supports my emphasis on the Bible's literary forms. While biblical themes are extremely valuable for probing the *dynamics* of the counselee's situation and making biblically informed *diagnoses* of it, the form enables us to focus on God's self-*disclosure* in the situation. Each literary form conceives God's self-disclosure in its own unique way. This fact enables us to foster the Bible's change agency by linking specific literary forms to specific situations addressed in pastoral care and counseling on the basis of the disclosive possibilities of the form itself. I do not, of course, claim that the Bible is a magic wand that need only be waved and God is instantaneously disclosed to us. Such a view would be hopelessly naive about God, and oblivious to the actual frustrations involved in achieving our care and counseling objectives. My point is simply that the Bible has a better opportunity to be disclosive, and thus a change agent, when there is a "good fit" between the biblical form and the counselee's personal situation.

As indicated, this fourth principle suggests a modification of the third principle. The third principle is now reformulated as follows:

3. *The principle of consistency.* This principle says that whatever use is made of psychological and psychotherapeutic theories and techniques in pastoral care and counseling, this use should be consistent with the disclosive power of the Bible. It is not that the Bible is conformed to psychotherapeutic goals, but that the use of psychological theories and methods is to be consistent with the disclosive possibilities of the biblical form being employed in shaping the care or counseling process. This way of putting the principle of consistency means that psychological and psychotherapeutic theories are not eliminated, for they can assist the pastor toward realizing the goals established on the basis of the biblical form. But it does give the Bible a very

22. Carl R. Rogers, "Perceptual Reorganization in Client-Centered Therapy," in *Perception: An Approach to Personality*, ed. Robert R. Blake and Glenn V. Ramsey (New York: Ronald, 1951); Capps, *Biblical Approaches to Pastoral Counseling*, 170–87.

central role in establishing these goals and shaping the counseling process.

This principle may seem to relegate theology to a secondary position to the Bible. But theology is not downplayed here, for this emphasis on the disclosive power of the Bible indicates that, theologically speaking, we are working with what Ricoeur calls "the idea of Revelation."

Conclusion

I realize that I have not given direct attention to the many practical issues this discussion raises. The fourth principle especially raises some critical practical concerns for pastoral care and counseling. If biblical forms shape the goals of pastoral care and counseling, how do they do this? Is this only a matter of pastors having such forms in the back of their minds as the counseling process unfolds or does the form need to be introduced in a more overt way, for example, counselor and counselee reading a parable of Jesus together? These are questions that deserve more careful consideration than is possible here, but certainly our four principles provide general guidelines for exploring these practical concerns. The fundamental principle in addressing such issues is the fourth principle. The question that needs to be foremost in the pastor's mind is how the Bible may become a change agent in this pastoral situation. This is the basic question, and the basis from which one addresses these practical issues.

One final but very important point is that in cases where the Bible is not introduced directly into the pastoral conversation, the four principles nonetheless remain applicable. If the biblical form is only in the back of the pastor's mind and no text reflective of that form is quoted or alluded to, the pastor still wants to be satisfied that the form *itself* is relevant to the situation, is sensitive to the limitations of the person being cared for or counseled, is an appropriate basis for goal setting, and is a potential change agent. Thus, the principles apply when the Bible is read or quoted, and they equally apply when the Bible informs the counseling process in a nonverbalized but no less intentional manner.

4

Incarnation and Pastoral Care

HERBERT ANDERSON

Incarnational theology has gained currency recently as a theological framework for thinking about the specialized pastoral work of care and counseling. The correlation of incarnation and care is one variant of a larger question regarding the connection between God's incarnation in Christ and our life, which is always body life. This essay is an examination of the usefulness of incarnation as a theological metaphor for pastoral care and counseling.

The question behind the question that prompts this essay is an old one: Where is the intersection between the human and the divine? The traditional Christian answer to that question is to point to Jesus. *Et incarnatus est.* Jesus is the incarnation of God—the enfleshment of the Word of God who was before the world began. That affirmation has never been easily understood. Christians have debated and continue to debate whether and how the divine and human meet in Jesus.

Major controversies of the Christian church have in one way or another revolved around differing interpretations of the Christ event. The Docetists said that Jesus only seemed to be human. Subsequent Gnostic formulations of that same principle despaired about enfleshment altogether. The Adoptionists took the opposite position. Jesus was fully human but adopted by God, or Jesus was regarded as a human, in the fullest sense, who was gifted with divine powers. Chris-

57

tological controversies throughout the church's history have been variants of those early debates.

The use of incarnation as a theological perspective for pastoral care does not seem to be occupied with any of these perennial controversies of the church. Frequently, the use of incarnational theology seems to point toward an approach to ministry that identifies the care-giver with Christ. One chaplain said it to me this way, "When I enter a hospital room, the body of Christ is my body." For that chaplain, incarnational theology provides a framework for embodying the love of God through daily care without necessarily relating the incarnating style with *the* incarnation of God in Christ Jesus.

The Incarnation as Event, Paradigm, and Principle

Considerations of the incarnation for pastoral work have generally taken three directions: the incarnation as event, as paradigm, and as principle. The recognition of the incarnation as event has led Eduard Thurneysen to view pastoral care as individualized proclamation. From this perspective, the central focus of pastoral work is to represent in the present the incarnation of God in the past. It is, therefore, important to use the traditional language of faith in order to translate a past event into the present.[1] The use of God language becomes a critical component of pastoral care and counseling.

The second use of incarnation in relation to the work of care views pastoral relationships as analogous to the Word of God made flesh in Jesus. Specialists in pastoral care and counseling use the incarnation as a paradigm to interpret their presence as embodying the presence of Christ with people in crisis. Charles V. Gerkin has modified this paradigmatic approach with an "incarnational style of tending to present life experiences."[2] Such a posture is intended to generate pastoral relationships in which the providential care of God is disclosed. The incarnation is the central paradigm for the work of pastoral care.

In the third variant of this motif in the pastoral care movement, incarnation is more than an event and more than a paradigm. It is a principle that describes how the Word continues to become flesh. In

1. Eduard Thurneysen, *A Theology of Pastoral Care*, trans. Jack A. Worthington and Thomas Wieser (Atlanta: John Knox, 1962). "Pastoral care is a conversation resting on a very definite assumption. It intends to be a conversation that proceeds from the Word of God and leads to the Word of God."

2. Charles V. Gerkin, *Crisis Experience in Modern Life* (Nashville: Abingdon, 1979), 37. "To tend one's experience in an incarnational style is to tend what occurs . . . within the hermeneutic of openness to the signs and symbols of the epiphany of God's disclosure in the events of everyday life" (321).

a recent essay, James B. Nelson contends that what is miraculous about the incarnation is not the "interference in the natural world by the supernatural but the authentic discovery of who we are."[3] Our bodies are the revelations of God's new heaven and new earth. If we cannot know the gospel in our bodies, then we cannot know the gospel at all. Incarnational theology moves toward a body theology in which Auden's lines become the norm: "Love God in the World of the Flesh: and at your marriage all its occasions shall dance for joy."[4] From this perspective, bodily experience is the starting point for theological reflection on pastoral acts of care.

Incarnational theology as body theology is a useful principle as we seek to reconstruct a faith that has been primarily shaped by patriarchal or sexist dualism as well as body/mind dualism. Any movement toward human wholeness in our time must of necessity include an understanding that bodies are part of a creation that God has labeled good. The belief that matter matters is one of the unique contributions of Christianity. For that reason, our spirituality is, of necessity, wedded to our sexuality. It is an incarnational spirituality. However, apart from the important recognition that every instance of care involves a meeting of body-selves—and hence we take body language seriously— the incarnation as principle does not directly illumine the pastoral work of care and counseling. However, understanding the incarnation as event and as paradigm is useful in addressing four interrelated questions often asked by the care-giver: Who am I in this context? How am I perceived by the recipient of my care? What am I doing here? Who is the other who addresses me in need?

Incarnation and Pastoral Identity

In response to the question "Who am I?" the incarnation as identification is the dominant motif. The specialist in pastoral care gains internal legitimation through identification with Jesus. If indeed my body is Christ's body, then my being in a counseling relationship or in the hospital room is authenticated through identification with Christ. Embodying Christ means literally that I understand my body to be a means of grace. The transforming love of God is made known by my presence.

Identification of my body with Christ's body is a powerful image

3. James B. Nelson, *Between Two Gardens: Reflections on Sexuality and Religious Experience* (New York: Pilgrim, 1983), 29.

4. W. H. Auden, "For the Time Being," in *Religious Drama I*, ed. Marvin Halverson (New York: Meridan, 1957), 68.

and an awesome equation that is at the same time too individualistic and too presumptuous. It is awesome in the sense that personal identification with Christ adds power and credibility to one's presence. There is power in equating my body with Christ's body. Whatever confusion of roles might exist for those whose pastoral ministry is carried out in the marketplaces of society, there is certainty in this identification with the incarnation. Moreover, being identified with the victorious Lord of death may soften the care-giver's sense of powerlessness in the presence of psychic chaos, family violence, or fatal illness. A pastoral care-giver is a sign of the transforming and humanizing presence of God. Equating one's body with the body of Christ means that the care-giver's being present is itself a mediation of God's presence where God sometimes seems absent.

While there can be no doubt that identification with Christ's body is a useful image for reinforcing the identity of the care-giver, by itself it is too narrowly an individualistic understanding of how Christ's incarnation is continued to our time.

It is the church that is identified with the body of Christ. And it is Christ who extends his incarnation through the church. My body is Christ's body *only* insofar as my life and ministry flow out of God's continuing incarnating through the church.

Because of the inescapably corporate character of God's self-disclosure, any identification of the pastoral specialist with the incarnation must of necessity point beyond one's particular body to the church, just as the church always points beyond itself to Christ. Incarnation as identification is always corporate. The Spirit of Christ that embodies the church continually seeks expanding embodiment in a community.

Chaplains and pastoral counselors, whose connection to the church is sometimes peripheral, may use incarnational theology to identify their bodies with Christ's body as a way of bypassing more critical questions of ecclesiology and pastoral care.

The church is called into existence by God to do God's work. It is, therefore, not simply a voluntary organization for the pursuit of human ends. Our pastoral work is dependent on the interconnection of two realities: the event of the incarnation and the reality of the church as the extension of that incarnation. The church cannot and does not exist except as the embodiment of Christ's body in the world today. Incarnation as identification is in danger of becoming a privatisitic approach to faith and ministry that is not consistent with the corporate image of body of Christ from Scripture. It would be useful to look at private pastoral practice from this perspective of the church as the extension of the incarnation.

There is a second critique of identifying my body and Christ's body that directly affects pastoral care. The patient in the hospital bed, the family in distress, or the individual immobilized by fear or over-whelmed by grief, frequently experience God as absent. In the midst of human pain and suffering, in the darkness of isolation and despair, God seems far away. The words of the psalmist and the cry of dereliction from the cross are frequently heard in hospital corridors and from people whose anguished cry pleads for a sign of God's presence. "Where are you, God? Why have you forsaken me? Why are you so far from me?"

In one sense, the identification of Christ's presence with the pastoral care-giver may be experienced as a tangible sign that God has not abandoned the patient to loneliness and pain. However, there is a danger that an incarnational theology that focuses on the mediating presence of Christ in the chaplain will dull the creative experience of God's absence. Christ's experience on the cross of God's abandonment was part of his incarnation. The assurance of presence prematurely given may short-circuit the painful but positive process of discovering the depths of human autonomy in the face of God's absence. If the chaplain embodies Christ, then God can only be experienced as absent when the chaplain is absent, making it difficult to sustain the patient through an experience of God's absence when the pastoral care-giver is present.

Incarnation and Ascribed Power

The second question to which incarnational theology is a response is less obvious but no less significant. How I am perceived by the recipient of my care is also a question of identity. It is not always predictable how others will respond to me. There is therefore always some risk on the part of the care-giver that his or her overtures will be misunderstood. Care is exaggerated into affection. Limit-setting becomes rejection. Sometimes, our efforts to incarnate God's care turn sour because our being for others is not enough. They want more than we are willing or able to give. And sometimes we are tempted to promise more than we can deliver.

Understanding God's incarnation has not been an easy matter, because from the beginning people have wanted Jesus to be more than he was. Those who were looking for a spectacular demonstration of God's power were disappointed that Jesus did not arrive according to a Cecil B. De Mille script. Those who looked for a political messiah who would overpower the Roman rulers came up empty-handed. Wandering about with uneducated fishermen, riding a donkey, and dying a criminal's death did not conform to the heroic expectations of a liberating messiah. How one is perceived by the other is a question that even in the life and ministry of Jesus points to perennial disappointment.

I would suggest that the image of incarnation as hero worship or heroic transference points to a basic human desire to make our helpers to be larger than life. In *The Denial of Death*, Ernest Becker has identified this impulse toward heroism as an effort to tame the terror of finitude. The making of heroes who are superhuman in character— who leap from tall buildings and know all the secrets of the psyche— is intended to create a buffer against death. Becker calls it transference heroics. In order to diminish the horror of isolation and smallness, the human creature seeks to merge with a greater power in order not to seem so small in the face of the vastness of the universe.[5]

By connecting with someone who is perceived to be larger than life, we modify our smallness and, for a brief moment, mute the terror of finitude. Being a personal friend of Jesus, a president, a counselor, or an electrifying preacher is a stride toward security. We expand our power by linking ourselves with those we have made to be larger than life. That's the good news. That's the reason transference is a pervasive human phenomenon. But there's a catch. We lose our uniqueness when we ascribe life-sustaining power to another. And so we must resist, especially those whom we have made our heroes. Resistance is a desperate effort to preserve individual uniqueness. "I can do to myself" is an emotional protest against the awareness that we lose our particularity when we ascribe power to helpers by making them larger than life.

Becker is correct. We cannot live without heroes. Our awareness of finitude is much too profound to be without buffers against the immensity of the cosmos and the capriciousness of death. "How am I perceived by the other?" is therefore a fundamental theological question. Incarnational theology provides a way for understanding a constructive role for heroics in human life. The incarnation deepens our own awareness of being human. The transforming power of the new Being—the incarnate Christ—sharpens the paradoxes of existence. The incarnating God to whom we point is a crucified God. God was not incarnate among us to take away our pain, but rather to enable us to live more courageously with the ambiguities of existence. No sweet Jesus here who covers over my struggles. Rather, the incarnation provides me with the courage to know the darkness and disharmonies of my life and endure.

The pastoral care-giver is often perceived to be larger than life.

5. Ernest Becker, *The Denial of Death* (New York: Free Press, 1973), 139ff.

People who are in distress, overwhelmed by their powerlessness or terrified of death, want us to have more answers than we know. They want our presence to be able to take away the terror of being small. They want to be assured that our prayers have more influence than theirs. They want us to promise that the pain will go away eventually and they will never again fear those things that go bump in the night. This is a perennial trap for pastoral care. There is something beguiling about being a buffer. And if we have already identified our body with Christ's body, we are in double jeopardy.

While we cannot shape how people will perceive us and respond to us, we can be sure that we do not believe it ourselves. That is not easy either. Being a buffer is itself a hedge against finitude. Being a hero is a protest against being small. That is the care-giver's dilemma. It is seductive to be regarded as larger than life. Sheldon Kopp, in his delightful book, *If You Meet the Buddha on the Road, Kill Him*, describes very accurately how people seeking help invest care-givers with superhuman wisdom and power and then sabotage it for fear of losing their uniqueness. "The patient will not have it any other way but that I am bigger, stronger, wiser than he is. I must rescue him, instruct him, teach him how to live. But Lord help me if I try. He will show me that in the long run my efforts are not sufficient, that he is not satisfied."[6]

We can all think about situations in which people have turned on us because we have failed to meet their heroic expectations. They did not want to see the darkness within. They wanted a bionic hero who would take away the terror and loneliness. On this matter, our identification with the incarnate Jesus may be a sobering reminder that God's way of being in the world does not whitewash creatureliness. Even Jesus died. The fundamental paradox continues. The human creature is a body who knows he or she will someday die. The human creature is at the same time a little lower than the angels and is food for worms. God's incarnation in Jesus did not take away that paradox. No amount of transference heroics will diminish the human dilemma of self-conscious finitude. But how we understand the incarnate Christ will affect the way we respond to those who would perceive us to be larger than life.

Incarnation and Pastoral Work

The third question, "What am I doing here?" shifts the focus from identity to action. Incarnational theology becomes a perspective for

6. Sheldon B. Kopp, *If You Meet the Buddha on the Road, Kill Him* (Palo Alto: Science and Behavior, 1972), 1–19.

understanding how our presence with another creates something new. Under this rubric, the incarnation is a paradigm for care. Christ's way of being in the world is a model or pattern for our way of being in the world in which care is the focus. There can be no doubt that our embodied presence is itself a significant dimension of care. It is being there for others that enables people to live through a terrifying surgery, a disintegrating marriage, or an agonizing loss. It is listening with our whole body to people who are plagued with doubt and fear and loneliness and grief. It is standing where they stand in empathy and understanding that modifies isolation and creates the possibility of something new. All of those images of being there for others, listening with the body, standing where they stand parallel the act of God in Christ. The care-giver's empathic understanding of another participates in the same ontic structures of empathic care as God's incarnation in Christ.

The kenotic image of the incarnation is a powerful paradigm for care. "Have this mind among yourselves," wrote Paul to the Phillippians, "which is yours in Christ Jesus, who, though he was in the form of God, did not count equality with God a thing to be grasped, but emptied himself, taking the form of a servant, being born in the likeness of men" (Phil. 2:5–7). The image of emptying is fundamental to God's incarnation in Christ. It is equally necessary for effective care.

Our way of being for others requires that we set aside our needs and desires. That is more what Luther had in mind in the passage from this treatise on the freedom of the Christian that is erroneously used to support the idea of being "little Christs." Here is what Luther says: "I will therefore give myself *as a Christ* to my neighbor, just as Christ offered himself to me: I will do nothing in this life except what I see is necessary, profitable, and salutary to my neighbor, since through faith I have an abundance of all good things in Christ."[7] The incarnation is a paradigm for care in the sense of empathy and embodied presence. It also provides a model for setting aside our needs for the sake of the other. It might be said that all care—whether human or divine—moves from emptying to embodying, and so to empathy.

Christ did not count equality with God something to hang on to. So also effective care depends first of all on the ability to set aside personal needs and desires for the sake of the other. It is an emptying in order to make room for the life of the other. This emptying makes embodiment possible. Otherwise we could not be "fully present" for the other in a way that parallels Christ being fully human for us. Our

7. Martin Luther, "The Freedom of a Christian," in *Luther's Works*, vol. 31 (Philadelphia: Muhlenberg, 1957), 367.

care is always embodied. It is in the flesh and with our bodies that we are present for another.

The ascension completes the incarnation paradigm. Christ's ascension means that God knows now in a way that God did not know before what it means to be human. Our humanity has been taken to the presence of God. Similarly, the care-giver's empathic response makes a similar understanding possible. From the patient's point of view, because of the care-giver's empathetic understanding "somebody knows in a way no one quite knew before what it means to be me." That experience of being understood is healing because it transforms our alienation and isolation.

While this paradigmatic approach to understanding the relationship between incarnation and care provides some guidelines for care, by itself it is of limited value for at least three reasons. First of all, there is no inherent reason to move from human processes of care to the transcendent reality of God. Structural similarity is not a satisfactory substitute for the liberating reality of God. Second, the incarnation, as paradigm, does not provide any recourse for us when our care falls short of the ontic structures of care that are incarnated in Christ. For example, it is not always possible for us to set aside our needs for the sake of others. Nor is our empathy ever as total and complete as God's becoming flesh.

The incarnation as paradigm does drive the care-giver toward an awareness of the grace of God that undergirds all feeble human efforts at care. While emptying oneself for the sake of the other is a fundamental preparation for care, it is humanly impossible to encourage the fainthearted and bury the dead indefinitely. It is humanly impossible to face an endless daily round of loose ends and injustices and despair. Emptying presupposes fullness. Those who care must themselves be repaired by the gospel of God, which brings life. And so the structural analogy breaks down. Human care-givers must themselves be cared for and filled up so that they can empty themselves again for the sake of others. God the incarnating one, is, however, never empty.

Incarnation and the Summons of the Other

So far, in our discussion, the pastoral care-giver has been the subject and the patient has been the object. The last question for which the incarnation may provide a perspective reverses that. "Who is the other who addressed me from the hospital bed?" is a question that makes the patient the subject. From a theological perspective, the patient or counselee summons my response as one for whom Christ died.

We do not ordinarily think about our perception of the patient as theological in nature. We are more often preoccupied with matters of identity and structures of care. When we focus on the patient, it is to determine the particular need of the one seeking help. The patient then is still object. We have, as a matter of fact, become preoccupied with determining the particular need of the patient in a minute way. Modes of care are then particularized to the needs of the cardiac patient or the ulcerative colitis patient or the adolescent leukemic victim or the grieving middle-aged son. Individualizing human needs is a way of insuring that we do not disregard the uniqueness of each child of God. Therefore, being attentive to the unique needs of each individual is itself a ministry of care.

Despite that attentiveness, the patient continues to be the object of care. From the perspective of incarnation theology, that must be reversed. In the sick or troubled one, we see our common, finite humanity. Incarnation as summons means that the other is the subject who calls forth my response. Although the familar passage in Matthew 25 is primarily concerned with identifying what kind of people followers of Jesus would be, it is also a powerful testimony to an understanding of the patient as one who summons response. "And the King will answer them, 'Truly, I say to you, as you did it to one of the least of these my brethren, you did it to me' " (Matt. 25:40). It is not that Christ is incarnated in the hungry, thirsty, or naked. Rather, Christ suffered the needs of suffering people and he—the incarnate one—is present with and in them. In feeding, clothing, and liberating them, we are ministering to Christ. They are signs pointing us to the one who, above all, labored and was heavy laden.[8]

The consequences of that shift for the practice of pastoral care could be remarkable. At minimum, it would mean that listening to the patient who is as Christ for me is theologically mandated. What is required for those who care is the ability to respond to the summons from the sick one who embodies for us all the suffering Christ. It may also mean that the recipient of our care becomes the subject who incarnates for us the gospel in surprising and vital ways.

8. Karl Rahner has understood the neighbor as Christ for me in a remarkable way. "To accept and assume one's human condition without reserve (and just who really does this remains uncertain) is for a person to receive the Son of man because in him [Jesus] God has received human beings. If Scripture discloses that he who loves his neighbor has fulfilled the law, this is the ultimate truth for the reason that God himself has become this neighbor, so in every neighbor we accept and love that one neighbor who unites what is nearest and farthest from us." Karl Rahner, S.J., "Jesus Christ," in *Theological Dictionary* (New York: Herder and Herder, 1965), 241–42.

Conclusion

We began by asking four questions that seemed to be addressed by incarnational theology. Each question has illuminated some convergence between incarnation and care as a way of understanding how the human and the divine meet in our time. We do not want or need a God who is withdrawn utterly from the world, but a God who is intimately involved with creation, who is connected with us where we live and where we struggle. For that reason, it is important that the incarnation be understood as a paradigmatic event that also compels us to action by identification or example or summons.

However, the depth of our urgency to connect God and care may cause us to assume that no such connection exists between a patient and God until we render care, until we provide the connection intentionally through our ministering, until we incarnate God for the patient by our presence. But this approach to incarnational theology, with its underlying assumption that God and the world are unconnected until connected by our incarnation ministry, does not take seriously the fact that the incarnation is a saving event as well as a moral event. There is but one incarnation in fact—that of God in Jesus the crucified. And it is in that incarnate one that God identifies with creation in order to make all the necessary connections.

The cosmic saving activity of God in Christ is eloquently described in the letter to the Colossians: "He is the image of the invisible God, the first-born of all creation; for in him all things were created, in heaven and on earth, visible and invisible, whether thrones or dominions or principalities or authorities—all things were created through him and for him. He is before all things, and in him all things hold together" (Col. 1:15–17). The connections between God and creation have all been made from the foundation of the world. Creator and creature are fundamentally, inherently connected because of God's love for what God has made. God's care for creation has already made the connections. This connectedness is affirmed, manifested, and embodied in Jesus.

What this means for pastoral care is that God has already incarnated himself for the patient or the troubled one before we enter the room. We are therefore free from the task of incarnating God, for that burden belongs to God who is the incarnating one. We do not bring God into a hospital room or the counseling relationship by our prayers or by our empathetic presence; nor do we incarnate God by our empathy. It is not for us to succeed or fail to connect God with our care by either our religious language or therapeutic actions. Our task is, more simply, to uncover the connections between God and the world, which already exist in Jesus. We still need to work at being present, making the connections, and establishing the rapport with those for whom we care, but we do that work in the confidence of what God has already done.

Our incarnation theology must finally lead us to the conviction that God is already present with the troubled one. Our being there is a way of pointing to and participating in God's saving incarnation. Because of the event of the incarnation, the encounter with the patient is already in Christ. The moment of care always points beyond itself—beyond our identity, beyond the structures of care, beyond even the summons from the patient, beyond our caring relationship to the incarnate one in whom we, the patient, and the relationship of care all have their being. We are free to care, knowing all the while that God the incarnating one has made all the connections from the beginning. In him all things—including our care for the sick—are held together.

5

Forgiving and the Christian Life

LEWIS B. SMEDES

A couple of years ago I asked a psychologist friend why psychologists had so little to say about forgiving. She answered: "Forgiving is a religious concept. We deal with understanding." I am grateful to psychologists for whom that dichotomy is unacceptable. I am grateful for psychologists around the country for whom faith can be a source of illumination on the human condition and on the possibilities for human healing. It is an affirmation of faith to say that forgiveness is God's invention for coming to terms with a past we wished had not happened, a past we cannot change or forget, a past that continues to lay its wretched reruns on the tender screens of our memories. It is precisely here that faith and psychology, or faith and therapy, are uniquely linked.

I have received much help from Erik H. Erikson. I read his works at a time in my life when I was trying to come to terms with some segments in my own history. I mention this because in spite of how much help he gave me, it was not enough to heal all the wounds that I inherited from the past. But I learned something important from him, and this is what I learned to the best of my memory. I am writing a story. It is my story and no one else's. More important, it is the only story that I can write; I have no other tale to tell. And the earlier chapters of my story are a final draft—no revisions, no editing, no blue pencil. I can only go on to the next chapter of my story, writing it out of the material that comes from the chapters already written. The irreversible realities of the early chapters become the grist for the unpredictable chapters of tomorrow.

Some things written in my early chapters I desperately want to change—the script that my parents wrote for me, the chapters that my children and I wrote together, some of my religious chapters, and certainly some of the bad choices that I have made. But there they are! I cannot change a syllable of my story, nor can I hold back the irreversible flow from the earlier segments as they pour into the chapters that I am writing now. God gives me only one story to write; it is my special story. There will never be another exactly like it, and I have to swallow the whole manuscript and build for the future on whatever God gave me in the past. I have learned to accept my past as my story, to be reconciled to myself and to the people who were fellow actors in the story.

This is what I learned from Erikson. And it came to me as one of those revelations of a simple truth that I knew all along. It was a precious and invigorating truth to me. Yet it is not enough.

Other people share my experience. Not everything in their past can be woven into their present and future. There are some scenes in our past that we just cannot use as the raw material for the chapters we want to write. They are lodged like undigestible lumps in the guts of our souls. They linger like unhealed scars in the membranes of our memories. We have to get rid of them, even if it takes some kind of divine intervention.

I had not fully realized until recently how many people carry a load of undigested lumps of brutally unfair experience. Painful memory keeps assaulting their present—moments when they felt let down by someone they believed was committed to them, moments when somebody treated them like strangers when they thought they were the dearest of friends, moments when they felt the sting of betrayal as someone they trusted treated them like an enemy. Or maybe they felt the dehumanizing assault of brutality when someone they trusted demeaned them with words or hurt them with brutal hands. They did not deserve the hurts—hurts that should not have happened, hurts that did not have to happen. It is for these insufferable wounds that God has invented the remedy of forgiving to supplement the freedom of acceptance.

As I tried to think about forgiving as love's revolution against unfair pain, I was surprised how little help I got from my fellow theologians. When theologians talk about forgiveness they almost always talk about how we can be forgiven by God and about what it takes for God to do that. I think this is partly why the churches are so much better at getting people forgiven than at helping people to forgive. But I did not get much help from psychologists either. So I was left on my own to pick up signals from here and there out of my own struggles and from people like me who were struggling to rescue themselves from their own pain.

The Forgiving Person

The first thing that I wanted to do was to get a handle on what a person does when he or she forgives somebody. I wanted to concentrate on what goes on in the heart and mind of the person who actually does the forgiving. I wanted to focus on the forgiver. I thought about the metaphors that the Bible uses and discovered that it always uses metaphors when it speaks of forgiving. I thought about what kind of situation could arise that makes this miracle necessary. What is the occasion for the crisis? I think the crisis is created by what I have already mentioned: by any past pain that we feel is unfair. It is created by a situation that is not only painful but wrong, not only bruising but unfair. It is not so much how deep it hurts but how wrong it feels that creates a crisis that can be resolved only by forgiving.

When we center on the person who is performing the minor miracle of forgiving, we observe at least four things going on. First, the person revises his or her vision of the one who hurt him or her. It is a revision of the vision. When someone hurts us unfairly and deeply, we almost always draw a caricature of that person, a bloated caricature in which we see him or her only as the villian who did us wrong. As the process of forgiving begins, however, we adjust our minds' aperture and see that person more truly as a weak, needy, and faulty person—not much different from us—who is coping with his or her own inadequacies by being cruel to us. The initial movement, then, is a revision of the vision.

Secondly, we heal our feelings toward the person. The change of vision becomes a change of feeling. The shift is not sudden, nor is it always clear, but gradually the moral fury inside us, the agonizing revulsion, the bittersweet taste of contempt, gradually recedes. We begin to feel a confused stirring of compassion, of care, of regret, maybe of concern. Feelings are mixed, and they always come in fits and starts. Few of us can drop our hate like we drop a hot pan. But still, almost as if on the sly, the changed vision brings changed feelings.

Thirdly, we surrender our right to get even. Everything in a decent soul's hunger for fairness tells him or her that he or she has a perfect right to fight back until the score is tied. There is nothing in the ordinary moral scale of values that can veto our right to retaliate when someone hurts us unfairly. But as we forgive, we gradually surrender that inalienable right to hurt him or her back. And the moral calculus that calls for a fair exchange is exploded by the violence of love, and we surrender and become free.

Finally, we wish the person well. We turn everything in the morality of natural humanness on its head and begin to feel a power to bless. Maybe it is negative at first—we just lose the sweet pleasure of imagining bad things happening to the person—but the satisfaction of imagining bad happenings gradually changes. Something more positive comes. We actually hope that he or she will do well. We actually pray that he or she will be blessed.

The climax of reconciliation, which sometimes follows forgiving, remains a possibility but only a possibility. Healing a relationship depends so much on the other person, on factors we can not control. Maybe the person we forgive will tell us to take our forgiveness and flush it down the toilet; maybe the person we forgive is dead; or maybe that person has become related to other people in such a way that she can no longer relate to us. Sometimes the hurting heart must heal alone. But the main thing is that now it is not our pain, not our hurt, that creates the gulf between us and prevents us from coming together.

Obstacles to Forgiving

Why is it so hard to forgive? That was the next thing I wanted to know. Sometimes it is hard because we are mean-spirited. We do not turn into saints just because we are suffering. So sometimes we do not forgive because we are sinners. But I think forgiving is hard for saints too. Maybe it was hard for God, I do not know. But it is not an easy role for even the most gifted forgiver to play.

I think at least two things make forgiving so hard. One of them is rooted in decent people's desire for fairness. When you forgive it seems as though you are letting the offender off the hook, as if it did not really matter that he or she did wrong. Everyone who smarts from unfair pain feels the unfairness of it: "She hurt me. I did not have it coming. Why should I have to forgive?"

I have never heard a case against forgiving put so powerfully as by a few people who responded to Simon Wiesenthal's story of his refusal to forgive a young SS trooper who was on his deathbed. Wiesenthal was a young architect at the time in a concentration camp in Poland. The Germans had improvised an old high school into a hospital to care for the wounded who were coming from the eastern front. One afternoon Wiesenthal was given the job of cleaning out the rubbish from the hospital, and a nurse grabbed him by the arm and said, "Come with me." She took him to the bedside of a young soldier who was going to die very soon. The young man clutched Wiesenthal by the wrist and said, "I had to talk to a Jew before I die. I had to tell a Jew some of the terrible things I've done. I had to be forgiven by a Jew." Wiesenthal listened and was silent for a moment; then he jerked his arm away and walked out of the hospital. The German died and went to God unforgiven by man. Wiesenthal was profoundly troubled. Did he do the right thing? His publisher asked several distinguished people what they thought. Most of them agreed with what he did. The philosopher Herbert Marcuse said, "People can not go around shooting innocent victims and expect to be forgiven just because they repent on their death bed." Cynthia Ozick, a brilliant Jewish novelist, was fierce: "Forgiveness can brutalize. . . . The face of forgiveness is mild but how stony to the slaughtered. Let the SS man . . . go to hell."[1]

I believe that almost everyone who feels the sting of unfair pain has at least a smidgen, maybe a bushelful, of the same reaction to unfairness that makes forgiving too much to ask. Forgiving seems to upset the natural sense for justice. What do we say, then, to the challenge that the very quintessence of the Christian life is unjust? Let me share two responses that I make to that charge, two insights that are helpful to me. Perhaps they will be helpful to you.

The first insight is that if you have been hurt unfairly, forgiving is the only way to be fair to yourself. Let us begin with the victim's rights. You have been hurt. The unchangeable fact is that you have been wronged, and you did not have it coming. Do you not have a right, then, not to be clobbered repeatedly with the same hurt in your memory? You have already been hurt once. Why should you go on experiencing the same hurt over and over again? Why not be fair to yourself? Why condemn yourself to be walloped in your memory by the same person who hurt you in the first place? How ironic that in the name of fairness you condemn yourself to a perpetual repetition of unfairness. I think people are mistaken when they believe forgiving is unfair to the forgiver. The person who gets the first payoff of fairness in an unfair world is the person who has mastered the miracle of forgiving.

The second insight is that the only way to create the possibility of less unfairness and of more fairness in the future is to cut through the unfairness of the present and open up possibilities. You cannot change the irreversible unfair past. You can only decide to make things more fair in the future. The alternative is to get even, but the fact is that

1. Lewis B. Smedes, *Forgive and Forget* (New York: Harper and Row, 1984), 126–128.

you can never get even. That is the irony and the tragedy. The person who causes the pain always weighs the pain on a different scale than the person who gets the pain. And when he or she receives it, he or she perceives it differently than you imagined. Why, then, shackle yourself to a nonstop, escalating unfairness? How many Catholics and Protestants will have to die in Ireland before the score is even? How many Palestinians or Israelis will have to die before there is a tie? The battle will go on eternally unless someone breaks in and, leaving the score uneven, tries to create a new beginning.

Forgiving opens up the possibility of getting out of the cycle of perpetual unfairness and onto the start of a new journey. The violence of love breaks into the circle of unfair pain, cutting the chain and opening up the possibilities, though never the certainties, of a fairer future. No, forgiveness is not unfair. It is love's unpredictable revolution for the creation of fairness in a world that is beset with pains and hurts that people do not necessarily have coming.

This is the best answer that I can think of to a question that I want to take with extreme seriousness. Whenever I talk to Jews who have been through, or whose parents have been through, the Holocaust and they say, "Don't come to us as a Christian and tell us to forgive. Don't come to us with your cheap forgiveness," I respect their reaction and try my best to deal with them honestly. I try to give an answer; I hope my answer is helpful to some people.

The second reason forgiving is so hard for us is that frequently we burden ourselves with misconceptions of what forgiving entails. Our bag of misunderstandings tends to make forgiving even harder than it needs to be. Three misconceptions deserve consideration here. First is the idea that to forgive is to forget. I think this is an unreasonable expectation. We do not have the power to stop our memories. Not even Jesus forgets. If you were to ask Jesus today, "Do you remember a fellow by the name of Judas Iscariot?" I do not think Jesus would say, "No! No! Never heard of him." He remembers. It is an unhelpful notion, then, and a dangerous one, in the second place, because there are some things we should always remember. To forget them is to let them happen again. The trick is to remember and still to forgive, and that is the hardest trick in the bag.

The second misconception is to say that to forgive is to tolerate what we have forgiven. The truth is the reverse: We forgive only those things we cannot tolerate. If we could tolerate them, we would not need to forgive them. A woman called me on a talk show one day and asked, "How do I forgive a drunk driver who last year ran over my four-year-old son and killed him?" Ten minutes later another call came in from a second woman. She said that the same thing had happened to her and that eventually she decided to do two things. She decided that she was not going to spend the rest of her life in hate, and, secondly, she decided to establish a chapter of Mothers Against Drunk Drivers. To forgive all is to heal ourselves; to tolerate all is to destroy ourselves eventually. I do not think people who tolerate everything are good forgivers. And I think that people who open themselves to being clobbered continuously ought to get their assailants off their backs before they forgive them. Forgiveness is not tolerance.

The third misconception is that to forgive is to excuse people. Forgiving is the opposite of excusing, for whenever you forgive you accuse, you sentence, you blame somebody. In distinction, you excuse people because you understand everything. The French say, "To understand all is to pardon all." This is not true. To understand all is to excuse all, to say that they are no longer to blame for what they did. But the forgiver says, "You are to blame, and I hold you responsible. I don't understand why you did it. You did not have to do it." And then the person forgives.

These are some of the misunderstandings that people load on forgiving. Beyond that, forgiving is difficult not only because we are often sour sinners but also because forgiving is so revolutionary, so unpredictable, so surprising, so unfactorable in the order of moral calculus that it seems unfair.

How to Forgive

We are now ready to consider how to forgive. To be honest, I do not have any instant recipe for forgiving. Every person must pursue his or her own pilgrimage. The best I can do is to set down some markers. Maybe some psychologists can find a technique for forgiving tucked away in their therapeutic toolbox, but I suspect that there is no easy formula. Anyway, let me suggest a few things that might be worth remembering.

I have three don'ts and a number of dos. First, the don'ts. First, do not ruin a nice miracle by turning it into an obligation. Forgiving is not a moral duty; it was not for God and it is not for us. We cannot factor it into a moral obligation, for it turns straight-laced moral systems on their heads. Morality says, "Get even"; grace says, "Forgive." Besides, I do not think that anybody in the history of human forgiving has ever forgiven because somebody told them they had to. Hurting people have asked me, "Why do I have a duty to forgive?" I respond: "Who said you had to?" God invites us to try his invention to see if it works for us. Incidentally, I think it is also wrong to moralize hate. Hate is nature's backlash against unfair pain. It is not wicked to hate.

I stand in awe of some people's righteous anger. The trouble with hate is that it is like cocaine. It feels so good that one does not want to let it go, but in the end it does the person in.

A second don't: Do not force forgiving into something you have to do at once. I am afraid of instant forgivers. Maybe there are five-star souls who can pull it off in a single feat, but fast forgivers may simply be rushing away from their own pain. Their quick-draw, shoot-from-the-hip forgiveness can be a device to deny their own hurt. Sometimes we are programmed not to feel soul pain. It is all right to feel physical pain but not to feel soul pain. I consider that a deprivation. I consider it too bad when people lose the ability to feel soul pain—just as bad as not being able to feel the pain of a burning arm.

I am also afraid that instant forgiving is an easy way to manipulate people. Instant forgivers misuse the word *forgive* the way they misuse the word *love*. They say "I love you" and what they really mean is "You turn me on and I want to use you." Just so, people can say "I forgive you" and what they really mean is, "You are the most contemptible cur that ever roamed the streetcorners of sinful humanity, and I don't want you to forget it." Quick-draw forgiving should not be encouraged.

The final don't is: Do not wait for the circumstances to be just right before you forgive. For instance, do not wait for a person to repent. If you are hurt you want the person who hurt you to grovel a little, but maybe he or she will not play your game and you may wait forever. You cannot control him or her. And if you wait for him or her to repent before you forgive, you may be giving him or her such power over your life that he or she, having hurt you once, can rob you of freedom and joy and healing for the rest of your life. For goodness sake do not wait for somebody to repent.

Now for some dos. First, I think a decision has to be made. We have to decide whether we want to wallow backstage with resentment or whether we want to dance on stage with freedom and healing. It is hard to make that decison—hard because hate tastes so wonderful that it becomes addictive. Hate creates beautiful illusions. The first illusion is the illusion of power. When you have been hurt, you can feel terribly weak or victimized or taken advantage of. When you hate, you feel as though you could lick anybody. Your contempt is the only weapon you have, so why should you let loose of it? The second illusion of hate is the illusion of virtue, the fantasy of goodness. I never feel as innocent as when I feel wounded without cause. The other person seems like such a demon, and I shine like a Virgin Mary in comparison. A hurting person feels virtuous. But when we hurt, we are usually not especially virtuous. So we have to decide, the way a cocaine sniffer eventually has to decide, what we really want. Do we want to live in the illusion of strength and the illusion of virtue, illusions that slowly turn us into sour and surly souls, or do we want to be free?

Second, it is important in the forgiving game to take our time. Most people cannot forgive in a single dip. Forgiving must often be done in increments, like opening up an IRA account—no instant bonanza but if you keep at it long enough you end up with substantial savings. I remember a letter that C. S. Lewis wrote about three months before he died. He said, "Dear Mary, I think I have at long last forgiven the cruel schoolmaster who so darkened my youth. I thought I had done it many times before, but now I really think I have done it." I'm sure he had. My guess is that had he lived, he might have had to do it again.

The third do is to limit our expectations of what will happen when we forgive. Some of us want to be healed, but we do not want to get too close to the person we forgive. We are reluctant to forgive, because we think that forgiving must end in an ecstatic embrace. It is good to remember that we cannot always turn the clock back and restore a relationship to its former state. Forgiving does not have to end with a climax of passion; we do not even have to like the person we forgive. So we can forgive and be healed without expecting it to end in a marvelous love story.

A fourth do: Be concrete, be specific about what the offender has done to you. We should not try massive mercy. God can forgive wholesale, but we have to be in the retail business. I think it is always good when we forgive to write down in verb form what we are forgiving, so we know what the person did. We should not use adjectives and nouns, because if we forgive in that way we will try to forgive persons for what they are. That is too big a lump for most of us to swallow, and besides, global forgiving is usually unfair to the person who is forgiven. It forgives a person for everything he or she is, which means that we may be forgiving them for aspects of their lives for which they are not responsible. So we should always forgive for specific offenses.

Fifthly, it is good to remember that we have to forgive in the midst of confusion. In the history of forgiving, nobody has ever gotten a totally accurate picture of just what happened to cause the alienation and the pain. Exactly who did what to whom and when and how and why will never be clarified. And it is just possible that if you say something to the person who hurt you, he or she might say, "Come on now, you are just too thin-skinned. What I did could not have hurt you that much." You may feel like telling him, "How do you know? You are too thick-skinned to know." The chances are that both of you will be half right. In any case it does not matter if you have exaggerated your pain or if in some eternal scale you had it coming. Objectively, it might be true that you do not have real reason or cause to forgive. The important thing is that you have a crying need to forgive. We are talking about healing, not about understanding. What matters is that you feel that you were betrayed or that you were brutalized, and you need to forgive. It is better to forgive when you do not really have to than it is not to forgive when you should.

In the sixth place, it is sometimes, not always, good to settle for implicit forgiving. Complete forgiving is always explicit forgiving— the person who forgives tells the person who is forgiven. But we do not live in a perfect world. Sometimes, therefore, it is good or necessary to leave the forgiving unspoken. Too much talk can get in the way. Several years ago I said something to somebody that deeply wounded two people whom I admired more than just about anyone else in my life. When my friends heard it secondhand, they were terribly injured and could not forgive me. We were alienated. For several years their wounded estrangement from me was a shadow that lingered over my life, and I would have done just about anything to have taken it away. Time passed. My friends forgave me and took me back into their lives. Our coming together is real and wonderful, but they have never said, "I forgive you." Why should they? I know they have forgiven me by their actions. Sometimes it is better this way. Sometimes it is better to do the act of forgiving. We need to be ready to settle for implicit forgiving.

Be content if you understand only part of the situation. If you understand everything about it, you do not need to forgive. And if someone has hurt you deeply, you are not going to understand anyway. Understanding only in part makes forgiving a little easier. Besides, the person who hurt you is probably not the devil he or she seemed to be. He or she is probably more like a weak, needy, and faulty human being who is trying to cope with his or her own weakness and in the process is cruel to you. If you can whittle him or her down to human size, you will find forgiving a little easier. I think it is true of the great monsters of history. They are giants at doing evil but are pygmies in their own breasts. And the fact is that you are not a superhuman saint either. Maybe your own foolishness was an accomplice to his or her unfairness. So blow away your own halo, and whittle his or her fiendishness down to size, and forgiving becomes easier.

The seventh do is prime the pump. Sometimes it helps to practice the symptoms of forgiving. It helps to suction up the waters of healing. If we say the words of blessing, "I wish him well. I wish him well," gradually the waters may start flowing. Praying also helps in mysterious ways. For one thing, it is embarrassing to ask God to bless someone when you want him to go to hell. Praying shames you into thinking differently. But the basic reason for praying is that God may just answer your prayers, both by blessing the person you are praying for and by giving you the miracle of being able to forgive.

Finally, we need to feel forgiven. If I as a minister wanted to ask people to forgive, the first thing I would do is to try to minister to them so they would feel forgiven. Feeling forgiven is much different from talking about it, from thinking about it, from knowing the doctrine about it. We can preach it and think about it and all the while walk around life with a black umbrella of guilt over our head. To help someone feel forgiven is to help him or her drown out the power of hate. I suspect in my own life that when I have felt forgiven, when I have felt that everything that I had ever done wrong was irrelevant and immaterial to how God feels about me, when I have felt that in and around and over me I was surrounded by a God who wished me only well, then I did not have the power not to forgive. Feeling forgiven and forgiving are so closely tied together that it is difficult to tell them apart.

Conclusion

This chapter is written to healers, to people who have given their lives to healing. I have written it on the assumption that at least some of you are wounded healers and that as you help people to forgive, you are working on your own life to set yourself free. Forgiving is love's tender violence, so unpredictable, so unexpected, so surprising, so healing in a world where innocent people hurt each other and bad people can hurt a lot. When we forgive, however, whether we are children or ninety-year-old persons, we tap into love's cosmic energy. We begin to ride the giant surf of love's great ocean. We walk in stride with God, and set the prisoner free only to discover that the prisoner we have set free is ourself. Most of all, we heal the hurt that we never had coming in the first place.

6

Forgiveness and Fulfillment in Pastoral Counseling

LeRoy Aden

Contemporary pastoral theorists frequently maintain that fulfillment of the self is the end point of pastoral counseling. They may even imply that fulfillment or self-actualization is a Christian mandate, that our faith asserts that in Christ God wills and works to enable us to reach our full potential. J. Harold Ellens, summarizing the position, suggests that "sin . . . is a failure in achievement of authenticity to self and of full-orbed personhood in Christ. It is a distortion and distraction to lesser achievements."[1] Ellens knows that we never achieve full personhood, that often we distort ourselves and live far below our potential. But he also believes that God's grace addresses our failure and he stands by to help us "achieve the self-actualization which expresses" our being a compatriot with him.

Ellens's position is a viable understanding of what the Christian faith says about our pastoral endeavors. After all, sanctification is an important dimension of God's empowering grace, and as Christians we are expected to help each other grow in our Christian life. Pastoral counseling is especially interested in self-actualization, partly because

1. J. Harold Ellens, "Biblical Themes in Psychological Theory and Practice," *The Bulletin* 6, no. 2 (1980): 5.

it sees the many ways that we fall into faulty fulfillment and partly because it knows that genuine fulfillment is a deep and constant longing of the human spirit.

In spite of the importance of fulfillment, I do not think that it is the end point or final goal of pastoral counseling. In fact, I believe that unless counseling transcends our preoccupation with fulfillment and begins to see forgiveness as its real end point, it contributes to rather than releases us from our deepest bondage—the constant attempt to make ourselves acceptable through what we achieve. This assertion rests on the assumption that fulfillment and forgiveness represent different understandings of the human situation in terms of both its problems and its possibilities. The two understandings may be interrelated, the one leading to the other, but fulfillment is not equivalent to nor can it be substituted for forgiveness.

Contemporary pastoral counseling has focused on the former to the neglect of the latter. In part, it has fallen into this error by following the lead of the psychological sciences, especially the lead of humanistic psychology, which tends to operate on the assumption that psychotherapy is to release individuals from their neuroses in order to help them achieve full and authentic personhood.

This assumption needs to be reexamined, especially in light of the Christian concept of divine grace. We can begin our investigation by looking at a particular theory of self-actualization. The possibilities are numerous (e.g., Kurt Goldstein, Abraham Maslow, Karen Horney, Frederick Perls), but the theorist who is succinct and has been the most influential in pastoral counseling is Carl R. Rogers.[2]

Rogers's Theory of Actualization

According to Rogers, human nature, at least its innermost core, is positive and constructive. Rogers calls this forward-moving thrust the tendency toward actualization. By this phrase, he means that given a proper environment people have an inherent tendency to fulfill themselves, to extend and develop all of their "capacities in ways which serve to maintain or enhance" their total being.

Rogers points to the infant as a naked instance of the actualizing tendency. He maintains that infants not only engage in activities that are intended to maintain or enhance their organism but also have the inherent capacity to evaluate these activities according to whether or not they are really fulfilling. Behaviors that are not fulfilling are seen

2. Carl R. Rogers, *On Becoming a Person: A Therapist's View of Psychotherapy* (Boston: Houghton Mifflin, 1961).

as harmful and are discarded. The implication of Rogers's position is simple but far-reaching. It asserts that infants have a built-in capacity to become whole and genuinely fulfilled persons. In fact, by their very nature they tend to become what they were meant to be, if they are not distorted by outside forces.

Unfortunately, infants are taken from themselves by "a natural—and tragic—development." In the process of growing, they gradually develop a self or a self-concept; that is, they begin to identify a portion of their total being and functioning as "I" or "me." The birth of the self is accompanied by "a need for positive regard." The child must feel that his or her presence and existence are important to others, especially to those who are important to him or her. In one ambiguous phrase, children need to feel loved.

This need, whether innate or learned, is as fundamental and as pervasive as the need for actualization. Its standard of evaluation, however, does not lie within the individual. It resides in other people, in how they respond to one's words and deeds. Children become attentive to this response. Consequently, they cease to judge a given behavior on the basis of whether it maintains and enhances them. Instead, another consideration, namely, how the behavior is valued by others, comes into play, and may become more dominant and determinative than the child's own organismic valuing process.

According to Rogers, the failure to follow the voice of the actualizing tendency is *the* tragic event in the life of the individual. The failure means many things, but above all it means the loss of one's destiny, the abandonment of what one should be and become. In our terminology, it means that the individual falls into a life of faulty fulfillment.

Rogers's whole therapeutic endeavor is an attempt to get individuals back to their "original state," back to genuine actualization. The centrality of this goal, and its exact meaning, come out into the open in Rogers's concept of the fully functioning person. Fully functioning people possess three interrelated qualities. First, they are open to the full range of their experience. Instead of eliminating all experiences that are incongruent with the self, the individual is "able to listen to himself, to experience what is going on within himself"[3] and to live that experience in its concrete fullness. Second, individuals are able to live in an existential fashion, that is, they are able to give themselves to the uniqueness and complexity of the moment. They live in the now of their experience, centered in what they are rather than in what they have been or in what they think they should be. Finally, individuals manifest a basic trust in themselves. They tend to do what feels right

3. Ibid., 188.

in the moment and find that their total organismic evaluation is a competent and trustworthy guide to contemporary behavior. When faulty decisions are made, fully functioning people are able to trust their second thoughts and to modify their behavior accordingly.

Rogers's preoccupation with self-actualization is not disconcerting to me, since fulfillment is a vital concern to us all. Likewise, his particular understanding of fulfillment is not a final worry, even though he does not seem to elaborate a fulfillment that is distinctively human. To put it crassly, with a little translation his fully functioning concept describes the life of a healthy amoeba as readily as it does the life of a healthy person, since amoebas, too, live fully in their present experience and trust their organismic reaction to it. What concerns me is Rogers's exclusive preoccupation with fulfillment, his unilateral emphasis on actualization in the face of our radically distorted existence. As a therapist, he has seen the agony and the consequences of faulty fulfillment at close range. He also knows the tenacity with which we hold onto our particular style of life.

These observations move Rogers in the direction of forgiveness, mostly in his concept of unconditional positive regard. He maintains that we get caught in our own "conditions of worth" and become free only when we receive unqualified "warmth, caring, liking, interest, respect." In this sense, unconditional positive regard, like forgiveness, seems to proclaim an acceptance that is received as a gift rather than one that is earned by achievement. The impression is misleading, for in actuality unconditional positive regard is radically different than forgiveness. The difference begins when Rogers assigns faulty fulfillment to a tragic inevitability, and not at all to personal guilt. He never uses the term *guilt* in his system. Individuals who are said to be distorted but not guilty may need to be helped back to proper fulfillment, but they have no need to be forgiven. The difference continues when Rogers gives unconditional acceptance a "because" character, and not an "in spite of" character. He maintains that individuals are accepted *because* they are unique and significant human beings. In contrast, forgiveness is unconditional in a total sense. It means that individuals are accepted *in spite of* being unacceptable. They cannot and need not measure up to any conditions that merit forgiveness. Not even the God-given quality of being a "unique and significant human being" qualifies them for forgiveness.

Rogers's unconditional acceptance, then, is not an exception to his preoccupation with actualization but a vital part of it. It represents one of the necessary and sufficient conditions that enable individuals to get back to their proper state—the optimal fulfillment of themselves. In this sense, Rogers epitomizes the contemporary tendency to absolutize fulfillment. He sees it as the end of, and the basic truth about, human life and designs his counseling to help individuals achieve their full potential.

Rogers's position is tenable as long as one holds, or at least emphasizes, an optimistic view of the human condition. It is more dubious if one takes seriously the persistent ambiguity and the final impotence of our lives. Then forgiveness, and not fulfillment, becomes an ultimate concern. Reinhold Niebuhr helps us to clarify the point.

Niebuhr's Understanding of People

According to Niebuhr, people are unable to live a righteous, let alone a fulfilled, life. Instead they are irretrievably in bondage to sin, that is, to egoism. Niebuhr's thought can be summarized by saying that persons can *envision* the unselfish but they can not *be* the unselfish.

Fulfillment, or to use Niebuhr's term *perfection*, refers to a balanced and creative expression of our bipolar existence as finite and free beings. It is possible only if we center our lives in God, who enables us to hold the two conflicting poles in proper and fulfilling balance. Unfortunately, this is only a "consummation devoutly to be wished," because the two strands of finiteness and freedom pull us in opposite directions, creating an internal condition of anxiety. We try to resolve the anxiety by our own efforts, primarily by denying our limitations and accentuating our possibilities.

The failure to perfect our essential nature does not destroy either that nature or our sense of obligation to it. No matter how distorted we may become, we still retain a vision of original perfection. Niebuhr believes that the locus of this vision is found in the capacity of the self to transcend itself. In other words, the self functions in different ways: "Sometimes the self acts and sometimes it contemplates its actions."[4] Niebuhr believes that the self in contemplation stands above its acts of thought and deed and becomes aware of its egoistic self-assertion. This awareness is a radical expression of our freedom and represents a creative and constructive use of it. It means that we can transcend ourselves and envision a mode of life or a pattern of behavior that is less egocentric. In a word, we are free to discover that we are not free. This is a moment of radical freedom, a moment when we have apparently suspended the operation of egoism.

At this very point—the point of our greatest freedom—our final and irrevocable bondage to sin is exposed. We are free in a limited but

4. Reinhold Niebuhr, *The Nature and Destiny of Man*, vol. 1 of *Human Nature* (New York: Charles Scribner's Sons, 1953), 259.

always in an ambiguous way. We fall "prey to the Pharisaic fallacy," that is, we assume that our "present ability to judge and criticize the undue and unjust claims of the self in a previous action is a guarantee of . . . virtue in a subsequent action." This pretension, which is itself an egoistic self-assertion, is manifestly false. According to Niebuhr, "when the self acts it always uses the previous transcendent perspective partly as a 'rationalization' and 'false front' for its" self-centered action.[5] In other words, every act of the self is inescapably colored by the taint of sin, where the word *act* is not limited to overt action but is used to refer to "every thought, mood, or action which proceeds from the self as anxious, finite, and insecure." In this sense, an act or the self in action is a qualitative dimension of every historical moment in the life of people.

The inescapable corruption of our noblest moments highlights the degree to which Niebuhr takes our bondage to sin and guilt. We can neither escape nor suspend the pernicious law of egoism, not even if we gain knowledge of its operation in a previous action. Egoism operates beyond the realm of conscious control as a defect of the will, which inevitably corrupts human existence. It is a quality of the whole person that touches every level and every act of the personality. This means that we cannot envision a larger community of justice without intruding the pretense that our scheme would ensure a greater degree of justice than the scheme of any other person. Likewise, we cannot pursue the truth without believing that our truth approaches the absolute. In short, we are able to *envision* the unselfish (the self in contemplation), but we are not able to *be* the unselfish (the self in action).

This intractable egoism is the quintessence of our impotence, making the achievement of authentic fulfillment impossible. No increase in the power or the scope of human freedom annuls this impotence, because "as freedom develops, both good and evil develop with it." Although increased freedom over nature and history opens up new possibilities for good, the law of egoism remains cogently operative. Thus "every new human potency" is turned into an instrument of disunity and destruction, every new increase of freedom into a greater and more subtle vehicle for egoistic self-assertion. In any one moment, therefore, we are powerless to make ourselves righteous, to free ourselves from the ravages of egoism.

Two Different Perspectives

It is apparent that Rogers and Niebuhr represent two different evaluations of our capacity to pursue genuine fulfillment. Rogers is opti-

5. Ibid., 277–78.

mistic; Niebuhr pessimistic. In the past, pastoral counseling has tended to go with Rogers and has operated on the assumption that fulfillment is the final, if not the God-mandated, end point of pastoral ministry. Niebuhr's understanding of people casts serious doubt on this position. It sees people as irretrievably bound to egoism and as incapable of actualizing genuine fulfillment. In fact, for him a step toward fulfillment is always a distortion of it.

If Niebuhr is right, we need to take forgiveness as a final goal of pastoral counseling far more seriously. It alone addresses and helps us to live with our persistent ambiguity and our final impotence. It locates ultimate hope not in our own afflicted achievements, but in God's unconditional acceptance. The result is both exhilarating and healing. It puts an end to our futile attempt to fulfill ourselves when that is not possible. It also corrects our tendency to locate our basic problem in the failure to achieve authentic personhood and helps us to see that we are in deeper trouble—that our turning from God and seeking to be the source and center of our own fulfillment is the root difficulty. We get caught in our own web. We are driven to measure up to a standard of perfection or a vision of optimal development that is beyond our power to achieve. The pursuit of fulfillment, then, is an endless and fruitless endeavor. The more we strive for it, the more it escapes us. Only an undeserved love that accepts us as we are can rescue us from constant frustration and feverish striving.

Forgiveness, then, and not fulfillment, should be the foundational perspective and the final concern of our pastoral counseling. This does not mean that fulfillment is eliminated as an end point, but it puts it in proper perspective: Fulfillment derives from and flows out of forgiveness. Or to reverse the paradox, forgiveness is fulfillment. By releasing us from the compulsive need to make something of ourselves, forgiveness frees and empowers us to be ourselves in a more authentic way than was possible before.[6] This fulfillment is never absolute, never unadulterated, so we always stand in need of forgiveness, but it is forgiveness that addresses our deepest need and heals our sorest malady. In this sense forgiveness is fulfillment. It represents acceptance when we are experiencing unacceptableness, freedom when we are caught in our own drivenness, wholeness when we are broken.

Forgiveness does not just put fulfillment in proper perspective; it actually recasts it in a different light. It shows that we are relational, and not self-contained, creatures. We are literally brought to life and restored in it, in and through relationships. For Saint Paul, this means that we are fulfilled not by seeking to actualize our own individual

6. See J. Harold Ellens, *God's Grace and Human Health* (Nashville: Abingdon, 1982).

selves but by expending ourselves in service to the neighbor in need. Paul, following Christ, turned away from the Greek idea that the goal of human life is the perfect development of individual personality and made serving others and promoting their welfare the essence of our nature. Paradoxically, then, it is by emptying ourselves, and not by pursuing our own ends, that we are fulfilled. Obviously, this represents a radical change in our understanding of human fulfillment, for fulfillment loses its autonomous, self-contained character and becomes the unselfish and loving action of serving others.

Forgiveness and Fulfillment in Action

The relation between forgiveness and fulfillment as end points of counseling can be clarified by a case study.

Jim and Joan come for counseling because their marriage is on the skids. In the initial interview, it becomes apparent that Jim is angry with Joan and sees her as immature and undependable. He even feels used and abused by her, especially when he finds himself picking up responsibilities that she drops. Underneath the surface Jim manifests an attitude of self-righteousness for being more mature and more dependable than Joan. He stands apart from her in obvious judgment and condemnation.

Joan labors under this judgment, feeling criticized and put down for everything she does. She tries desperately to do things in a way that might please Jim. No matter what she does, however, she cannot win. Her many efforts only aggravate the problem—for Jim because he feels that her efforts are forced and not spontaneous; for Joan because she is so concerned about doing the right thing that she makes foolish mistakes.

Jim and Joan's situation can be seen from different angles. Seen from a therapeutic perspective that considers fulfillment as its end point, their situation becomes a question of how to help the two of them find a better and more satisfying life. Improving their relationship is primary, of course, only as long as it is assumed that marital accord will enhance the fulfillment of each party. If that proves to be untrue, the counselor may alter his or her goals and work to enhance the fulfillment of each person apart from marriage.

In either case, the procedure is roughly the same. Insight-oriented therapists will seek to increase the self-awareness of both Jim and Joan. Initially, they may focus on the present and help the couple to examine their relationship so that they have a better and clearer picture of how they are relating to each other. In this endeavor, the counselor may make suggestions to the couple, or may even invite confrontation between them, in order to rework the relationship. At some point, the counselor will focus on the past and hope to uncover at least some of the repressed historical roots of Jim and Joan's behavior—all in the name of increasing their self-knowledge so that they are not blindly repeating repressed experiences and unknowingly reading them into present relationships. The assumption, valid in itself, is that if the couple knows why they are behaving as they are, they are in a better position to modify their behavior.

Specifically, this means that Jim must become aware of the compulsive and inordinate demands that he puts on Joan, demands that in part are projected onto her out of his own unconscious sense of inadequacy. He must also reexamine his tendency to pick up responsibilities that are Joan's and must realize that in his own way he is perpetuating her immaturity. Finally, he needs to plumb the depth and destructiveness of his self-righteousness and see that he is more limited and Joan more adequate than his condemnatory attitude grants.

Joan, on her part, must acknowledge her dependence, maybe even her need to be helpless and inadequate. She must come to know the extent to which she distorts and desecrates herself by trying to earn Jim's acceptance. Finally, she needs to get in touch with her anger, maybe even her rage, at Jim, at her parents, at herself, and at the God who seemingly made her less than adequate.

Jim and Joan need to become aware of all these things, and more. Their increased awareness will help them to become free of their chains and will empower them to live a more open and fulfilling life. The relationship between them will also improve, and they will find life together more satisfying. If therapy achieves these changes, it is to be applauded for having produced necessary and significant results.

Without casting aspersions on therapy's achievements, pastoral counseling with its theological rootage brings an added perspective to the situation and raises a question about ultimate results. First, it raises a question about the basic healing power of increased self-awareness. Jim and Joan will, one hopes, become more aware of their past motives and deeds, and this increased awareness may help them to become more understanding of themselves and of each other. But increased awareness by itself will not necessarily heal their hurts and disappointments and self-righteous judgments. In fact, it may aggravate and deepen them, for now they see the underside of each other more clearly even as they may heighten their expectations of the other person.

Increased awareness must lead beyond itself. Only if the therapeutic process helps Jim and Joan to forgive themselves and each other will they be released from the hate and self-righteousness of past hurts.

Jim, for example, may come to see why Joan is immature and irresponsible (e.g., because her parents overprotected her), but unless he is able to forgive her for her limitations and to accept her as she is, his resentment toward her or her parents will manifest itself in hidden and not-so-hidden ways. In similar fashion, Joan may come to see what Jim's condemnatory attitude has done to her, but unless she is able to forgive him she will continue to be imprisoned in his self-righteousness and will repeat its effects in relating to him.

Whatever is achieved, pastoral counseling sees that the healing is not absolute and once-for-all. Thus it raises a second and more radical question—a question about the nature of healing itself. Can Jim and Joan be released from their deepest malady and therefore move toward unadulterated fulfillment, either individually or together? Pastoral counseling sees the achievement as ambiguous at best. It may grant that the couple can be released from its historical chains, but it would not grant release at a deeper level where existential/ontological conflicts eventuate in egoistic self-assertions. There is no cure at this level—and no possibility for genuine fulfillment. What is needed, therefore, is a word of forgiveness, the assurance that one is accepted in spite of being unacceptable so that in the same spirit one can accept the other person even though he or she remains unacceptable. Andras Angyal calls it a sense of humility—the ability to admit the bankruptcy of one's former ways and to discard one's neurotic compensations and pretenses.[7] If Jim and Joan can live in this spirit, then they are able to accept themselves and each other and to find a kind of fulfillment that transcends both autonomous striving and the necessity to measure up to certain expectations. They are free to be themselves, and to allow each other to be himself or herself, in the quiet recognition that both are human and can be accepted and loved for who and what they are.

Conclusion

We have explored the possibility that forgiveness, and not fulfillment, is the end point of pastoral care and counseling, especially if we take seriously a Pauline understanding of the human condition. The full implications of this assertion for pastoral care are not immediately apparent. They will have to be explored at another time. Two points, however, need to be made from the outset. One, while forgiveness may be basic in pastoral care it does not eliminate fulfillment as a primary

7. Andras Angyal, *Neurosis and Treatment: A Holistic Theory* (New York: Wiley and Sons, 1965), 260.

concern. I have emphasized forgiveness in this article to try to correct an exclusive preoccupation with fulfillment, but in actuality both are important foci in pastoral ministry, just as they are important and complementary dimensions of God's grace. God both pardons and empowers, both acquits and gives new life. This twofold activity must be reflected in our pastoral care and counseling.

Second, forgiveness, however basic, is not an instant cure-all for what ails troubled people. Nor is it an immediately actualized possibility in most cases. Instead it participates in, and is distorted by, the personal and interpersonal dynamics of people; therefore, it often becomes effective in their lives only as they deal honestly and extensively with the specific details of their situation. In other words, forgiveness becomes a reality in the same way that fulfillment becomes a possibility. In both cases, the specific ways in which we have distorted life must be held up to critical self-examination, and we must become receptive to God's power to heal beyond our ability to merit it.

7

The Minister as Moral Counselor

JAMES M. GUSTAFSON

In 1949, my wife and I served as summer staff in a two-point parish northeast of Billings, Montana—Musselshell and Melstone. I cannot take time to describe either this area, half the size of Connecticut, or the people, few as they were, who lived there. A short time before we arrived an incident had occurred in Musselshell, where we lived, a village of about 120 people. A member of that congregation (I will call him Joe) had "whipped" another man on the gravel street between the post office and the little general store. The fight was to keep a vow. Earlier that spring, the loser in this fight had been let off by the judge in Roundup, the county seat, for an offense against a relative of Joe's for which Joe thought he should have been punished. Joe had vowed to the offender that if he ever showed his face in Musselshell, he would "clean his plow." The solemn vow had been fulfilled when the offender dared to appear.

Later in the summer, Joe came to me with a problem of conscience. Someone, unnamed, had put up five hundred dollars (a lot of money in those years, and more in Musselshell than some other places) to anyone who would clean Joe's plow. Another resident of the area came up from the bar, run by one of Joe's brothers, with the following proposition. The two of them would go out behind Musselshell in the Bull Mountains for a period of time, and they would come back to town looking like they had had a severe fight. Joe would look worse, and acknowledge that he had been whipped. They would split the five hundred dollars. Joe's question was the primal question of moral life, "What ought I to do?" That is a different question from "What is beneficial for me to do?" or "What do I feel like doing?" The question was, "What is the morally right thing for me to do?" It was not only a matter of finding what was morally right; it was also a matter of resisting temptation. In effect, it was an effort to understand some applicable principles of moral conduct that would resolve the matter of conscience, and be strong enough to govern his "will." Joe refused to join in this plot.

My impression, which might be distorted, is that a great deal of counseling, pastoral and otherwise, is oriented toward relieving anxiety, stress, and overburdening senses of guilt. In contrast with this, serious attention to moral matters can often increase anxiety, stress, and the sense of guilt. If the "ought" has a claim upon a human agent and upon the course of action he or she chooses, it often runs counter to what that person desires to do. It is also my impression that many people seek the aid of a counselor only after some action has taken place or some event has occurred that disturbs them deeply. I have no strong evidence for this, but to reiterate my hunch, I suspect fewer people seek counsel on the basis of asking "What ought I to do?" than seek counsel when they are disturbed about what they did, and thus ask "Did I do the right thing?" I know that not all of pastoral counseling deals with moral matters, that is, with matters in which an intention determined an action of moral significance and in which the person can be attributed with causal and moral accountability for the consequences. A lot of it deals with events beyond one's control, like the death of a person for whom one grieves. A lot of it deals with a sense of misplaced accountability for events and consequences, and thus misplaced guilt.

This initial spading around has dug up only some of the complications involved in the area of my interest. There are philosophical, theological, and other dimensions that can be easily exposed. Joe's resolution, for example, might be expressed in the following terms: His essential being, what he truly was, was the ground of his conduct. The problem of conscience was merely a matter of getting his existential being in a coherent relation to his essential being. Thus, what was the right thing to do was what he most deeply desired to do, and so the *ought* and the *is* were happily in harmony. What he ought to do was what he most deeply wanted to do, and thus a morally happy ending. But the reverse, from a moral standpoint, is often the case: what a person most deeply wants to do is not always what a person ought to do. It might well run counter to obligations one has undertaken in promises and vows; it might violate some natural duties that one has as a member of a family, or the rights of another person. We might fiddle with abstract terms in such a way that in some ideal sphere, or presumptive real sphere, the discord between desire and ought is resolved, but there are many instances in which this is not helpful, and may even be a rationalization, in the worst sense, to justify the mitigation of the force of moral duties and obligations one has to others. One can find excuses, if not good reasons, to justify all sorts of conduct.

Let's go back to Joe. He was the father of two sons for whom he had high aspirations. He did not have regular employment; the trade he was best equipped to do was carpentry, and there was not much to be done in Musselshell County at that time. His house, like the one in which we lived, did not have running water, while that of one of his brothers near by and a number of others did. If one reckoned the prospective consequences of the proposal made to him, the weight of benefits from his consent was considerable. He might have had a bad conscience for awhile, but then he might come to his pastor, or simply take it to the Lord in prayer to get forgiveness. What was morally wrong were not the possible consequences, but that the proposal involved deceit. Deceit was morally wrong not because deep in his heart Joe believed it was morally wrong. Deceit would have been morally wrong whether Joe thought it was wrong or not. To be sure, it can be argued that there are extreme circumstances in which deceit is excusable. To refer to one of the oldest and most famous examples in Western moral literature, if deceit would save the life of a person, some moralists, but not all, would justify it. Kant would not. Vindicating reasons can be given to show why deceit is morally wrong. One might be that it is proscribed in Joe's case, by inferences drawn from two commandments of the Decalogue: "You shall not steal," and "You shall not bear false witness against your neighbor." Another might be that if one generalized or universalized permission to be deceitful, the fabric of human relations would simply fall into disarray. If Joe had consented, he would have been objectively guilty of an objective moral wrong.

While my story is surely exceptionable in its details, in its more general point it is not. Deceit is a common phenomenon. Moral philosophers argue about whether there is ever a genuine moral dilemma. If one has the correct moral theory, some argue, there is never a dilemma; every conflict of prima facie duties or claims can be resolved rationally. This is not the place to argue for or against various moral theories, and of course the philosophers have not yet persuaded each other, but if we begin with the perceptions of moral agents, of persons, they are often faced with conflicting moral claims. Some occasions occur in particularly critical times: families are consulted about the continuation of high-technology life supports in hospitals. Others are more common: adolescents are bombarded with various pressures about sexual conduct; men and women are torn between obligations to their children and requirements of their occupation; the claims of the needy for our disposable income conflict with desires we have for more comforts and conveniences for ourselves; complex social and political issues are not easily resolved, and the like.

My perception, which may be inaccurate, is that a great deal of pastoral care is directed toward relieving persons of the burdens of anxiety, stress, and guilt that various experiences engender in people. If there is a theological basis for this it is the one I have heard over and over in sermons, namely, that "you are accepted." Nothing one has done can separate one from the love of God. The prime metaphor is healing, and thus the prime diagnosis is illness, and the metaphor of illness tends to mitigate the sense of accountability that people have for their conditions. Illness, after all, usually is something that happens to a person, not something he caused and therefore for which he is morally accountable. Moral theologians and pastors can become very adept at relieving distress by providing causal explanations of it that view the person involved more as a patient than as an agent, more as the object and victim of forces beyond the person's control than as the agent whose choices have created certain difficult conditions and as agents whose future choices can avoid some such conditions. Explanations of behavior and circumstances provide morally excusing conditions. Even if I am only partially correct in this perception, I want to note that the struggle between moral rigorists and moral "laxists" is an old one in the church, and that clearly there have been excesses at both extremes.

Blaise Pascal was a Jansenist rigorist, and his *Provincial Letters* give us some of the most hilarious satire in the history of theological literature, satire directed to the Jesuit laxists of the seventeenth century. The letters are in part conversations between a penitent and a laxist confessor. I commend the reading of the *Letters*, and take time to illustrate only from a small portion.

"Show me, with all your directing of intention," returned I, "that it is allowable to fight a duel."

"Our great Hurtado de Mendoza," said the father, "will satisfy you on that point in a twinkling. 'If a gentlemen,' says he, in a passage cited by Diana, 'who is challenged to fight a duel, is well known to have no

religion, and if the vices to which he is openly and unscrupulously ad-
dicted are such that would lead people to conclude, in the event of his
refusing to fight, that he is actuated, not by fear of God, but by coward-
ice, and induce them to say of him that he was a hen, and not a man;
in that case he may, to save his honor, appear at the appointed spot, not,
indeed with express intention of fighting a duel, but merely with that of
defending himself, should the person who challenged him come there
unjustly to attack him. His action in this case, viewed by itself, will be
perfectly indifferent; for what moral evil is there in one stepping into a
field, taking a stroll in expectation of meeting a person, and defending
one's self in the event of being attacked? And thus the gentlemen is guilty
of no sin whatever; for in fact, it cannot be called accepting a challenge
at all, his intention being directed to other circumstances."[1]

I will not entertain you more; the account goes on for many more
pages in which Pascal has the priest quoting from the moral theologians in such a way to justify killing. Of course, the key in this is
always one's intention; one is not simply finding excusing conditions
but defining intentions in such a way that things that are prima facie
morally wrong turn out to be morally approvable. We moderns, and
particularly we Protestants, are not as adept at analyzing intentions
and their objections as were these seventeenth-century Jesuits, but we
are quite skilled at showing the limitations of human accountability
for human actions, and thus can provide excuses that relieve the burdens of anxiety and guilt. We can quickly invoke the forgiving love of
God, and underplay the law of God. We do that in modern times not
because we are worried about "works-righteousness," not because we
have a theological principle that states that our relation to God cannot
be earned by moral merits.

I am not interested, however, in making indictments; but rather to
turn attention to some suggestions about what the role of the moral
counselor might be and what some of the implications for theological
education might be.

First, the minister as a moral counselor is not a prescriptive role,
except perhaps in the most extreme circumstances. When one reads
pre-Vatican II manuals of moral theology, one does find casuistry ex-
ercised to very prescriptive conclusions about very particular acts.
Protestants are also very prescriptive about very complex matters in
the pronouncements they pass in such large numbers on issues of
morality and social policy. Contrary to a prescriptive role, I imagine
that of a moral counselor to be one in which the minister finally honors

1. Blaise Pascal, *Pensées and Provincial Letters* (New York: Modern Library, 1941),
406–7.

the conscience of the individual, but by asking relevant ethical questions and providing relevant information, the individual can come to an ethically considered judgment about a course of action. Asking ethical questions is important; and it is in part to ask the person questions she or he has not asked, or would like to avoid asking. However, a choice is not morally conscientious if people have not considered, or been provoked to consider, the moral reasons that would go counter to their apparent wishes and desires, as well as those reasons that would sustain them. Moral counseling is not like writing a resolution in which the preferred judgment is sustained by a series of "whereases" of selected evidences and principles without accounting for evidences and principles that might lead to a different judgment.

I want to use a brief example from a time in which many of us acted as moral counselors, namely, to the 1960s and the early 1970s when students were subject to the draft. Without doing a survey, I certainly found that a lot of "draft counseling" amounted to clergy and others generally affirming choices for nonparticipation in one of several ways: continuation of student deferred status, and avoiding the hard consequences of a clear moral choice; preparation of good grounds for conscientious-objection application; or the radical moral action of refusing to register. There was also a lot of draft counseling that would meet standards I have in mind. Some questions were these:

> What reasons would you give for the Vietnam War being without a just cause?
>
> What reasons and evidences do you adduce against particular arguments that the cause is just?
>
> Why do you think it is fair for you to be deferred or exempted on any grounds when others are subject to conscription?
>
> With reference to student deferment and theological student exemption particularly, have you really made a conscientious moral choice when you have been able to avoid the consequences of such a choice that others have had to endure?

I could go on to remind us of the questions asked about the grounds for conscientious objection, and particularly to test the integrity of the objection. But my point with reference to this example, and more generally, is that moral counseling involves *interrogation*. Interrogation sounds harsh because we usually think of it in terms of police and courts; it does not necessarily carry that weight. Interrogation procedures are a necessary element of moral counseling. The best result that can come from them is that the person resolves an ambivalence, and/or has good reasons for the choice that is finally made. The choice will be a genuinely conscientious one.

What I have said needs nuance and embellishment, and obviously the particular circumstances and the particularities of the person involved need to be taken into account.

Four dimensions are required, in my judgment, in pastoral moral counseling. We begin with the ought question. Our concern is what capacities and resources are needed to help persons answer the ought question conscientiously.

1. What constitutes an adequate description and analysis of the circumstances in which the ought question comes up? For my parishioner Joe, they are not especially complex; for the student seeking help about the draft in a particular war, they are more complex. Since we answer the ought question in part on the basis of our understanding of the circumstances, understanding involving both information and analysis, there must be some tests of the adequacy of that understanding. It is what I call an evaluative description; that is, judgments are made about what matters are morally relevant, and what kind of configuration one gives to them, but the practical import of the inquiry is that often we make moral errors because we misperceive, misunderstand, or are misinformed about the circumstances.

2. What ethical issues have emerged beyond the simple ought question, and what concepts and principles are required to think ethically about them? For example, in the case of Joe, as I developed it, the issue was one of deceit. The question then becomes how we think about deceit, and why it is morally right or wrong to engage in it. In other examples it might be a matter of fairness or justice; in others it might be how to judge the human values that will be affected by the probable consequences of various courses of action. What is required is capacity to use ethical concepts properly.

3. Who are the principal agents involved in the action, and what makes them the sort of moral people they are? My conversations with Joe would have been quite different if I had not known that he had a strong sense of moral integrity, a moral strength that others in the same circumstances might not have had. With the draft illustrations, we were concerned about strength of convictions as well as reasons for them, with possibilities of self-deception as well as deception of others.

4. What religious and theological convictions back and inform both the counselor's and the person's moral outlooks and practical

reasoning? Even in the interrogation process the sorts of questions and how they are asked are affected by the minister's religious viewpoint, and if the other person is serious about religious life and faith, they matter for him or her as well.

Preparation to deal with each of these dimensions draws on aspects of seminary education. I simply call this to your attention without elaboration because I think the implications are quite clear. What, in my impression, is not widely done in seminaries is training people to draw various resources together in a moral counseling way. The process is partly one of casuistry, though classically casuistry is the application of principles to cases. Moral counseling includes casuistic thinking, but as I am proposing it the prescriptive tone of some casuistry is not involved.

Now I turn to the following case.

A couple in their late thirties makes an appointment to see you. The wife is pregnant; it is her first pregnancy and they have desired to have a child for some years. Her physician has told them that the odds that they will have a genetically defective child increase greatly after a woman's thirty-fifth year. Particularly, he indicated that she is more likely to have a child afflicted with Downs Syndrome than is a woman much younger. He has told them that she can undergo amniocentesis; the analysis of the results of this procedure will indicate whether the fetus has Downs Syndrome and/or a number of other defects. If Downs Syndrome or other defects are detected, they have the option of inducing an abortion.

The couple is not sure what they believe morally about abortion, and the information they have received has put a note of anxiety into their joy about the wife's pregnancy.

What information do we need to have to engage in responsible counseling of this couple? We need to know more than they did about genetic diseases, and particularly about Downs Syndrome. Also, we need to know more about amniocentesis and even about abortion.

To answer the question of what ethical issues the situation of the couple raised, it is necessary to make certain distinctions and to learn to use certain ethical concepts. In this case the principal matter is the possibility of aborting a fetus. If the fetus was diagnosed as genetically defective, the parents were faced with that choice.

The abortion issue provides an opportunity to explore not only the more obvious issues that are widely known, but also to analyze various ways in which people, including professional ethicians, think about and resolve ethical questions. For example, one can ask whether a defective fetus, assuming one can determine what counts as a defect, has a right to life. This introduces a way of thinking (i.e., a rights-based ethics). It is not necessary to be deeply informed about deontic ethics, its history, and its major supporters, but as a way of determining what actions are right, certain assumptions and procedures of deontic ethics can be explored. An alternative is to think axiologically, which is to ask the question of the value of fetal life, and how values can be discriminated. Consequentalism is an other alternative; should the couple think about this in terms of the probable consequences of aborting or continuing the pregnancy? Consequences for whom? How does one determine good and bad consequences on the basis of good reasons? Thus, it was necessary for the ministers to learn some things, or retrieve some things they had learned, about various ethical theories. If a conscientious choice follows from having good reasons for it, it is important to help people understand what constitutes good ethical reasons. This requires that a vocabulary be learned and that people learn to use certain concepts.

The third area of questions concerns knowledge about the prospective agents involved in the decision. The pastor might know the people well enough to understand both empathetically and according to some principles of interpretation much that is required to see what their prospective choice means from the ways in which they live and view the world. Surely something of their life histories and the stories that shape their valuations is important to know. There will be differences in capacities to cope with adversity, and thus some probabilities can be assessed about potential outcomes of alternative choices. Even if this knowledge is not decisive in settling the moral question, it is important in the moral counseling process. It is essential to inquire about the "psychodynamics" of making a difficult moral choice, but also what other aspects of the moral character, experience, and outlooks that the people had.

The last area is that of inquiry about the religious convictions and theological outlooks of both the pastoral counselor and the parishioner. The task in this fourth area is not to find some theology that supports an ethical predisposition. Instead the task is to be clear enough about what one believes to see how certain moral choices follow from those beliefs. The counselor must be clear about his or her own religious convictions, and help others to formulate and articulate their beliefs.

Certainly there are many ways to go about training ministers to be moral counselors. A case study is only one way. My aspiration is that this approach provides a starting point from which to think about how moral counseling, as an aspect of pastoral care, might be developed in the training of the ministry.

8

Pastoral Counseling and Moral Change

LeRoy Aden

The ability of counseling to effect significant change in the interpersonal and intrapsychic dimensions of an individual's life is an accepted fact in many professional circles today. Firsthand experience either with counseling or with someone who has been through counseling has helped to establish the fact. On a more disciplined level, men like Carl R. Rogers have made an undeniable contribution. Out of an intense and systematic study of counseling, Rogers and his followers have been able to pinpoint some of the major directions and end points that result from an efficacious therapeutic relationship.

Counseling as an instrument of psychological change, then, is being established and elucidated. Unfortunately, the same cannot be said of counseling as an instrument of moral change. In fact, since the days of Sigmund Freud most psychotherapists believe that moral issues, and especially moral judgments, impede rather than promote the therapeutic intent of a counseling relationship. Although this position embodies a great deal of clinical wisdom, it has had the unfortunate effect of discouraging serious study of the relation between counseling and moral values. This neglect leaves unexplored a persistent datum of my experience as a pastoral counselor. It ignores the fact that the counseling process often seems to bring about a noticeable and significant change in the moral dimension of a person's life.

In the present chapter, I want to pinpoint some of the significant effects that counseling seems to have on the moral behavior of individuals. Though the effects are not an automatic outcome of counseling, they seem to be a frequent occurrence whenever genuine change has occurred in the individual's personal and interpersonal life. In fact, clinical experience indicates that the change educed by counseling is unitary and wholistic, so that any change that is manifested in the moral dimension of a person's life is actually part of a larger whole.

I will set forth and elaborate three propositions that seem to be descriptive of the moral change that occurs when counseling promotes significant growth.

Moral Perception

First, the individual's moral perspective tends to become more comprehensive and inclusive.

The moral perception, especially the moral self-perception, of individuals in the early stages of counseling tends to be shallow and unilateral. People tend to perceive themselves and others from an absolute perspective, applying a hasty and categorical label of good or bad to acts and feelings that are actually complex and ambiguous. Clinical examples are abundant. Joan, the mild-mannered, self-effacing spouse of a chronic alcoholic, says, "I'm loaded with resentment. I hate him, and that's bad, isn't it?" Forty-year-old John, having lost all love for his devoted wife, confesses in bewilderment, "I want to love her, at least I feel I should love her. This apathy, this not caring is not good, not right." Finally, a single woman named Mary who underwent an induced abortion to terminate an embarrassing pregnancy lives with the feeling, "It's like I can never get past what I did. It's just like a gate or something. I can't get beyond it. I'm guilty; therefore I'm condemned."

Each of these instances illustrates the tendency of clients to see their behavior from a position of selective awareness. They judge their thoughts or deeds from a narrow perspective, failing to see or to explore the larger context of their moral action. This shallowness may reach unbelievable proportions, mostly because people may perceive themselves from some part-process that has been absolutized. For instance, the clinical examples indicate that individuals may see and judge themselves from the standpoint of a single deed or desire. In other words, it is possible for one experience to become so decisive for individuals that they tend to perceive themselves from the vantage point of that experience alone. This is the radical extent to which the moral perspective of a beginning client may be unilateral and un-realistic.

Counseling helps to correct an individual's moral myopia by in-creasing his or her awareness of the factors that are involved in any moral action. Heinz Hartmann elaborates the point:

> In analysis, man is confronted with a more encompassing reach of "his good" and "his bad" than he has been aware of before. . . . The confron-tation with the unconscious mind, the undoing of the blind spots, as to the "good" as well as the "evil," can give to moral awareness a depth dimension that it would be lacking otherwise.[1]

In other words, counseling tends to do for moral awareness what it does for awareness in general. It expands and deepens it, making it much more open to the total situation of the individual. In terms of morality, this means that individuals come to see that their moral behavior is not an isolated part of their personality, that moral action is never simply a product of moral values or ethical ideals. On the contrary, it is a dimension of the total person, and therefore it is re-lated to and influenced by many different life factors—factors that are conscious and unconscious, past and present, personal and interper-sonal, moral and nonmoral. To be adequate a moral perspective must be open to these and other factors that are significant in any given situation.

Increasing the individual's moral awareness is an important accom-plishment in a twofold way. In a minimal sense, it is essential to a proper and adequate understanding of one's moral behavior, for the meaning of that behavior can never be divorced from the factors and forces that help to create it. The point is illustrated by a client who terminated counseling with the feeling, "The things I have done don't seem so horrible anymore, because I know why I did them." This statement should not be distorted to mean that the individual has slid into an antinomian morass where all moral judgments are eliminated. Instead she is pointing to the suspension of a radical and naive self-condemnation. Her moral self-perception now includes a historical depth and a cross-sectional breadth it lacked before, and with this increased awareness she is able to see her behavior in its larger context and to appraise it more realistically. Instead of getting stuck on the level of mere labels, she is able to see and understand some of the actual dynamics that contributed to her behavior, not in the name of

1. Heinz Hartmann, *Psychoanalysis and Moral Values* (New York: International Universities Press, 1960), 94.

justifying her actions but in the name of comprehending and owning them more fully.

In a more foundational sense, the expansion of moral awareness, like the expansion of awareness in general, means that the person is less subject to the operation of unconscious determinisms. According to Rogers, important experiences that are denied or distorted often operate as hidden determinisms of behavior. These determinisms can and often do influence the person's moral behavior, usually in a vicious and unwholesome way. A woman suffers from a trend toward morbid dependency, and as a result she is nudged toward an illicit and guilt-ridden extramarital affair. A man's need to feel secure and powerful tempts him to embezzle large sums of money and to live a life of deception and dishonesty. A teen-ager, tired of struggling against a sense of emptiness, takes life into his own hands and seeks to crush it. Each of these instances illustrates that genetic determinisms of an interpersonal or intrapsychic nature can have and often do have significant moral consequences. Counseling indicates that these consequences tend to diminish as the individual becomes less driven by and more free of the unconscious determinisms that support them. An increase in the individual's awareness of and release from the deterministic forces is therefore an important and basic event in his or her whole life, including his or her moral life.

Moral Response

Second, the individual's moral response tends to become more authentic.

The moral response of individuals in the early stages of counseling tends to be spurious and even moralistic because it proceeds out of what they think they ought to do or be rather than out of who they actually are. Dietrich Bonhoeffer's description of the Pharisee is to the point: "He is the man to whom only the knowledge of good and evil has come to be of importance in his entire life; in other words, he is simply the man of disunion. . . . Every moment of life becomes a situation of conflict in which he has to choose between good and evil."[2] In other words, Pharisees subordinate their lives to a knowledge of good and evil and judge themselves and every situation in light of its unyielding demands. We would say that they are split down the center of their existence. This split, in the moral sphere of life, manifests itself as a compelling need to fulfill certain legalistic dictates no matter

2. Dietrich Bonhoeffer, *Ethics*, ed. Eberhard Bethge (New York: Macmillan, 1955), 26ff.

what the person may really desire. The dictates may derive from others or self, from past or present, but whatever their origin, they represent norms or expectations that are extraneous to the individual's contemporary authenticity. They are "an external will imposed upon us, an arbitrary law . . . [that] is strange to our essential nature."[3]

Mr. Delta, a thirty-six-year-old father of two children, married his young wife shortly after he returned from military service. The thought of her possible unfaithfulness tortured him in unguarded moments, but he dismissed it. After all, his wife came from a good home, she seemed happy and satisfied as a wife and mother, and he on his part was quite attentive to her needs and wishes. It came as a shock, therefore, when one night his wife confessed to him that she had recently carried on a six-week affair with an old high-school friend. She had terminated the affair out of fear of being caught and wanted to tell him the real facts before he heard the story secondhand.

Mr. Delta followed his first impulse. He pressed divorce proceedings to their final stage before he was persuaded by parents and friends that his wife had made a "little mistake" and that he should try to forgive and forget. Mr. Delta's next impulse was to beat the third party "within half an inch of his rotten life," but here again he was persuaded to remain within the bounds of reason and be civil about the whole affair. Thus under the strong pressure of parents and wife and for the sake of his children, Mr. Delta tried to wrench his hurt and hostile thoughts back into a form that was decent and respectable. He succeeded amazingly well. "I shouldn't detest my wife for her unfaithfulness" gradually covered up the less desirable feeling that "she stabbed me in the back and cannot be trusted," and "I am not reasonable when I have the impulse to kill the other man" became a socialized substitute for the deeper feeling that "he should be made to pay for what he did instead of being free to prance around the community without a blemish." In each case, Mr. Delta has come to live by the dictates of a social ought. The feeling of what should or should not be the case takes precedence over what really is the case, so that what may seem like moral maturity is really an artificial construct that is alienated from his real, and in some sense, legitimate feelings.

Counseling tends to take the spurious and the artificial out of the moral behavior of persons. It moves them away from a morality based on fixed precepts toward a morality that is based on their own inner existence, on what they have been in the past and what they are in the present. This movement is not, as one might suspect, a movement toward an undisciplined and lawless subjectivity. It is much more

3. Paul Tillich, *Morality and Beyond* (New York: Harper and Row, 1963), 24.

positive than that. More specifically, it is, if it is genuine, a new understanding of oneself as a moral person coupled with a renewed capacity to actualize and live according to one's own deeper nature.

From the perspective of pastoral counseling, the phrase "a new understanding of oneself" means that individuals gain a deeper understanding of their moral plight. They begin to see that their plight is not just a matter of obeying or disobeying particular laws and, concomitantly, that they are not released from their plight by trying to fulfill the demands of a commanding conscience. In a word, they discover that the command to be good neither makes them good nor gives them the power to do it. In fact, the more goodness is demanded of them, whether by internal or external law, the more intense their moral plight becomes and the more likely they are to fail. In this sense counseling, especially pastoral counseling, helps clients to get beyond the level of law to a more adequate level of morality. It helps them to see through the fallacy and frustration that is involved in any final preoccupation with pharisaic failures or successes. Consequently, individuals begin to struggle with the underlying quality of their whole life, for they begin to see that true or genuine morality is a qualitative thing, involving the totality of their being. For them, then, moral action emerges from who they are instead of coming out of some rigid or superimposed structure. It is a product—a genuine and natural product—of the individual's whole being.

Morality in this sense is authentic, for it refers to the actualization of one's potential self. It is a genuine fulfillment of one's true being rather than "blind obedience to an external law, human or divine." Counseling often helps individuals become moral in this sense, not as an achieved condition but as a direction of development. Their moral response becomes more authentic insofar as they gain an increased capacity to respond to, and to live out of, the accrued summation of who they are.

Increased Trust of Moral Decision and Evaluation

Third, the individual becomes a more trustworthy locus of moral decision and evaluation.

In the early stages of counseling, individuals tend to operate with the locus of decision at the periphery of their existence, either in some code of moral law or in some part-process within their own lives. This tendency is not without good reason. As a divided rather than a centered self, the individual's decisions and evaluations are not a reliable reflection of his or her total being. Consequently, the person is not a trustworthy judge of what is and what is not genuinely fulfilling. Counseling tends to correct this situation. By returning individuals to themselves, it makes their responses more organismic and therefore more trustworthy. They become the best evaluator and determiner of their own moral action, because they are the ones who possess the deepest and greatest knowledge of what is for them genuine morality or authentic self-fulfillment.

The point can be taken a step further. Counseling not only increases the trust of individuals in their moral decisions and evaluations, but also increases their trust in themselves as moral persons. When individuals first come for counseling, they tend to feel that if their defenses were lowered they would be swept along by intense and uncontrollable desires to carry out various kinds of destructive and antisocial behavior. Contrary to these initial expectations, individuals often discover that their organismic desires are not evil or immoral. In fact, when they are open to their deeper needs and desires they move in a positive and constructive direction, not in the sense of obeying every demand of the social law, but in the sense of seeking to actualize what is genuine fulfillment for self and others. In theological terms, we are dealing with the essential and God-created goodness of persons, and on this level we are saying that an individual is a moral creature and can be trusted to act in a moral way.

This positive evaluation of our moral nature becomes an empirical fact as counseling approaches the point of being maximally successful, but it is only half of the story. Successful counseling does not necessarily show that evil is epiphenomenal to humankind's basic nature. If anything, it shows that human nature is ambiguous at best, a mixture of good and evil. Freud came to the same conclusion: "If any one were inclined to put forward the paradoxical proposition that the normal man is not only far more immoral than he believes but also far more moral than he has any idea of, psychoanalysis, which is responsible for the first half of the assertion, would have no objection to raise against the second half." In an explanatory footnote Freud clarified the meaning of the proposition. "It simply states that human nature has a far greater capacity, both for good and for evil, than it thinks it has, i.e., than it is aware of through the conscious perception of the ego."[4] Counseling helps individuals to see both dimensions of their being, so that they begin to appreciate their goodness and their badness to a previously unknown depth.

The awareness of one's moral ambiguity adds a final dimension to our discussion. As individuals become more aware of their ambiguity,

4. Sigmund Freud, *The Ego and the Id*, trans. Joan Riviere (London: Hogarth, 1927), 75–76.

they find that trust in themselves as moral persons is not enough. Seeing the depth of their moral failure, the guilt that they feel for doing or being what they should not have done or been intensifies a need that has been present since the beginning of counseling—the need to get beyond a crippling sense of judgment and condemnation. In other words, they need to gain a genuine sense of forgiveness, a sense of being accepted by God in spite of being unacceptable. Counseling, especially pastoral counseling, often helps to achieve this goal. As individuals progress in counseling, their ability to experience and to accept God's forgiveness increases, while the burden of a destructive and sometimes spurious sense of judgment tends to decrease. They begin to see themselves in a much more charitable light, because they have a deep sense of being accepted and forgiven by a gracious and loving God. This change, which comes as a gift, also gives them increased power to use the resources they have to move toward fulfillment, however partial and ambiguous that fulfillment may be. In a word, it increases their ability to be moral persons in the context of trusting God and attempting to do his will.

Conclusion

Counseling can be and often is an instrument of moral change. More precisely, we can say that as counseling approaches the point of being maximally successful, it produces significant personality change. This change is manifested in the moral sphere of life, primarily by making the individual's moral perspective more encompassing, the individual's moral response more authentic, and the individual's ability to be the locus of moral action and the object of divine forgiveness more responsible. Each characteristic is a vital and essential contribution to morality in the deepest sense of that word, that is, to morality as authentic fulfillment of one's God-given personhood within a community of individuals.

9

The Psychodynamics of Christian Conversion

J. HAROLD ELLENS

In *The Transforming Moment*, James E. Loder attempted to illumine our understanding of "convictional experiences" in human life.[1] He thus contributed to the current preoccupation with parapsychological phenomena, described by him and others as significant spiritual experiences. Aside from the complexity and frequent obscurity of his book, Loder begs the question of the nature of spirituality throughout.

Launching his argument from a traumatic personal experience of temporary paralysis following an auto accident, the author interprets as a distinctive spiritual phenomenon what seems quite clearly to be the remission of a classic hysteria reaction. The book unsuccessfully attempts to describe the watershed that distinguishes subjective psychological process from true spirituality and personalized divine intervention in human life.

Loder's book makes one useful contribution. It illustrates the excesses to which some serious Christians are tempted in their anti-intellectualism, their reaction to the psychologizing of spirituality, and their often naive but endemic antipathy to positivist empiricist epistemology.

1. James E. Loder, *The Transforming Moment* (New York: Harper and Row, 1981).

The primary problem with this posture is its tendency to denigrate the legitimate domains and contributions of the social sciences, out of apparent anxiety that those sciences will consume and eclipse theology and spiritual authenticity. A responsible Christian perspective, however, undoubtedly requires that phenomena that can be accounted for satisfactorily by the psychological model, the physics model, the sociological model, the geological model, respectively, and the like, ought so to be accounted for and ought not to be spiritualized. That is merely a proper contemporary application of Occam's razor. Theology and spirituality, where they are authentic and ring true to experience, can, no doubt, stand on their own feet.

Structuralist Models

For that reason the structuralists in personality development theory offer more than spiritualists like Loder. James W. Fowler offers a thoroughly digested statement of the structuralist view of psychosocial development as applied to growth in faith and spirituality.[2] It illumines Loder's convictional experiences and transforming moments without denigrating or truncating psychosocial theory or data. Fowler assumes the legitimacy and usefulness of Jean Piaget's model of cognitive development, Lawrence Kohlberg's model of moral development, and Erik H. Erikson's model of psychosocial development.[3] He correctly perceives that these three models are not in tension but mutually illumine and elaborate each other. Tables 4–7 briefly present the stages of each of these models of human development.

Fowler's Main Contribution

Fowler presents a taxonomy of faith development stages and characteristics that corresponds to, illumines, and completes the spiritual side of structuralism. His taxonomy appears in its most refined and mature form in his *Stages of Faith.*[4] Table 8 presents an integrated picture of his model of faith development.

Fowler's work moves to one point: the manner in which people come to focused and redemptive meaning, faith, agapic love, freedom,

2. James W. Fowler, *Stages of Faith* (New York: Harper and Row, 1981).
3. Jean Piaget, *Six Psychological Studies* (New York: Random, 1967); idem, *The Psychology of the Child* (New York: Random, 1969); Lawrence Kohlberg, "Education, Moral Development and Faith," *Journal of Moral Education* 4, no. 1 (1974); idem, "Moral Stages and Moralization," in *Moral Development and Behavior*, ed. T. Lickona (New York: Holt, Rinehard and Winston, 1976); Erik H. Erikson, *Childhood and Society* (New York: Norton, 1963); idem, *Insight and Responsibility*, (New York: Norton, 1964).
4. Fowler, *Stages of Faith*.

Table 4 Fowler's Development Stages

Years	Stage
0–2	Infancy
2–7	Early Childhood
7–13	Childhood
13–21	Adolescence
21–35	Young Adulthood
35—	Adulthood/Maturity

Table 5 Piaget's Cognitive Development Stages

Years	Stage
0–2	Primarily Sensorimotor
2–7	Preoperational and Intuitive
7–13	Concrete Operational
13–21	Formal Operational: Dichotomizing
21–35	Formal Operational: Dialectical
35—	Formal Operational: Synthetic

Table 6 Kohlberg's Moral Development Stages

Years	Stage
0–2	Response to Positive and Negative Reward
2–7	Preconventional: Heteronomous Morality
7–13	Preconventional: Instrumental Hedonism
13–21	Conventional: Mutual Interpersonal Concord Law and Order Morality
21–35	Conventional: Social System Priority, Conscience Dominant, Class-biased Universalism
35—	Postconventional: Social Contract, Individual Rights, Principled Higher Law
(60—)	Universal Ethical Principles, Loyalty to Being

Table 7 Erikson's Psychosocial Development Stages

Years	Stage
0–2	Basic Trust vs Mistrust: Hope
2–7	Autonomy vs Shame and Doubt: Will Initiative vs Guilt: Purpose
7–13	Industry vs Inferiority: Competence
13–21	Identity vs Role Confusion: Fidelity
21–35	Intimacy vs Isolation: Love
35—	Generativity vs Stagnation: Care
(60—)	Integrity vs Despair: Wisdom

Table 8 **Fowler's Taxonomy of Faith Development by Ages, Stages and Aspects: A Comprehensive Structuralist Model**

Years/Stages	A (Piaget) Form of Logic	B (Kohlberg) Form of Moral Judgement	C (Erikson) Form of Psycho-Social Function	D Bounds of Social Awareness	E Locus of Authority	F Forms of World Coherence	G Symbolic Function
0–2 *Infancy*	Primarily Sensorimotor	Respond to Positive or Negative Reward	Basic Trust vs Mistrust; Hope	Family, Primal Others. Significant Object Relationship	Attachment/dependence Relationships Size, Power, Visible Symbols of Authority	Fragile, Episodic, Vacillating	Magical Numinous
2–7 *Early Childhood: Intuitive and Projective*	Preoperational and Intuitive	Preconventional: Heteronomous Morality	Autonomy vs Shame and Doubt: Will / Initiative vs Guilt: Purpose				
7–13 *Childhood Mythic-Literal*	Concrete Operational	Preconventional: Instrumental Hedonism	Industry vs Inferiority: Competence	Like Self in Family Social and Religious Terms	Authority Figures Based upon Personal Relatedness	Narrative Dramatic (Histrionic)	Literal one-dimensional
13–21 *Adolescence Synthetic-Conventional*	Formal Operational: Dichotomizing	Conventional: Mutual Interpersonal Concord, Law and Order Morality	Identity vs Role Confusion: Fidelity	Composite of Group in Which One Has Interpersonal Relationships	Consensus of Valued Groups of Worthy Representatives of Value and Belief System	Tacit System, Felt Meanings, Symbolic, Global Import but Clear Boundaries	Symbolic, Multi-dimensional Progress from Symbol Adherence to Meaning Commitment

21–35 Young Adulthood Individuative-Reflexive	Formal Operational: Dialectical	Conventional: Social System, Reflective Relativism, Conscience, Class-biased Universalism	Intimacy vs Isolation: Love	Ideologically Congruent Communities and Self-Chosen Norms	Own Convictions with Self-Ratified Ideology Authority and Norms Judged on Congruency	Multi-system Symbolism and Concepts	Post-critical Reunion of Symbol and Meaning Reality Perceived Beyond Both
35— Adulthood Paradoxical-Consolidative	Formal Operational: Synthetic	Post-Conventional: Social Contract, Individual Rights, Principled Higher Law	Generativity vs Stagnation: Care	Disciplined, Ideological Vulnerability to Other's "Truths" or "Claims"	Open to Dialectical Interaction with Other Perspectives on Human Wisdom and Worldviews	Unity in Experience and Concept	Exocative Power of Truth and Reality Experienced in Unification of Symbol, Symbolized and Self
(60—) Maturity Universalizing	Formal Operational: Synthetic	Post-Conventional: Universal Ethical Principles, Loyalty to Being	Integrity vs Despair: Wisdom	Identification with Species. Trans-Narcissistic Love of Being	Commitment to Intuition, Principle of Being, and Personal Judgement		

peace, Christian hope, and an inspiring sense of the presence of God. The distinctiveness of his approach over against that of John Westerhof is crucial.[5] The latter assumes that people are merely *socialized* into the experience of faith by the believing community. It is merely a matter of "straight line" growth, dependent for effectiveness upon the quality of the expectations and perspective of the environmental community. Fowler recognizes that despite the communal environment and running through the socialization is an inherent structural process, native to the person, which mediates the effectiveness of psychosocial and spiritual development and growth in the faith.

Donald M. Joy recently offered a vigorous and thorough critique of the structuralist model.[6] He attempted to carve out a larger space for the supernaturalist function of the Holy Spirit. His book returns to the notion that special forms of divine intervention in human life, faith, and growth transcend such "humanist" notions as structuralism and its evolutionistic implications. Such special divine interventions come in the form of the varied human experiences of conversion. The critique is interesting but falls short of its mark. Finally, its implied reversion to the fundamentalist heresy of the two worlds, God's supernatural world and the other world of natural experience or natural/social sciences, fails to credit adequately the psychosocial model and demeans spiritual faith and experience as esoteric phenomena. Moreover, Joy seems to have overlooked Fowler's concept of faith, conversion, and the ministry of the Holy Spirit.

Structuralism and Spirituality

Fowler's concept is complex but may be summarized as follows. People achieve Christian faith by growing up into it. That growth proceeds through the cognitive, moral and psychosocial stages of Piaget, Kohlberg, and Erikson. Daniel J. Levinson's contribution is also illumining. As growth proceeds through the stages it opens persons to the needs and potential patterns characteristic of each stage. The content of the spiritual growth at each stage will depend significantly upon the information, attitudes, values, and faith commitments of the environmental community, as well as upon the personal experience patterns and events in the subject's life. Those experiences, whether traumatic or pleasurable, may be constructive or destructive, depending upon how they are integrated. Integration depends upon the inherent pattern of the stage at which the experience is received, the

5. John Westerhof, *Will Our Children Have Faith?* (New York: Seabury, 1976).
6. Donald M. Joy and others, *Moral Development Foundations, Judeo-Christian Alternatives to Piaget/Kohlberg* (Nashville: Abingdon, 1983).

perspective of the community, and the information level of the person. Christian conversion is an integration process or event that sets the whole in a perspective that allows faith and God's grace to function as the center and ground of meaning, purpose, hope, and relationships. If Christian conversion takes place as a dramatic reintegration event, it often produces a recapitulation or reprocessing of all the prior stages of a person's growth and regrounds one's orientation, values, and virtues in the "light of faith's new center of value, images of power and decisive master story. . . . When the recapitulative process has done its work, the person has a new foundation of inner integration from which to move decisively toward the next stage."[7]

The work of Professor J. E. Massey suggests that humans frequently experience arrested growth at one of the adult stages. Massey argues that adults continue to grow largely as a result of "significant emotional events," which stimulate movement to the next stage.[8] Perhaps, in fact, this may be a clue to the trigger mechanism of movement to growth at each stage of life: significant emotional events being generated by inner-need dynamics as well as by outer stimuli.

In any case, the external stimuli that frequently trigger growth in adults, moving them to the next cognitive, moral, psychosocial, or spiritual stage, seem to come in one of three forms. A "significant emotional event," perhaps otherwise identifiable as a significant event in the psyche, may be a new insight, a new relationship, or a new trauma. These represent events at the cognitive, psychosocial, and moral-spiritual levels of knowing and experiencing, respectively. The event is significant in size or value when it is "life shaping," when it provides a new or renewed sense of meaning, perspective, and being.

The Thesis

It is the thesis of this chapter that the dynamics at work in the "significant emotional event" are approximately as follows. When a person experiences a significant new life-shaping insight, relationship, or trauma, that event-experience cuts through all of the structures and defense processes of the personality structure or developmental formation and reaches all the way down to the characterological level. There, at that level, the cognitive, psychosocial, and moral-spiritual content of the "significant emotional event" produces a paradigm shift in the value and belief system. The assumptions, commitments, loves, values, or beliefs that have heretofore constituted the ground of being and integrating perspective are now all illumined in a new way with

7. Fowler, *Stages of Faith,* 290–91.
8. J. E. Massey, *You Are Where You Were When,* videotape series, Boulder, Colo.

the new light of the new "significant event of the psyche." As in the shift of the visual pattern in a kaleidoscope as one turns the barrel two degrees or more, so also at the value and belief level of the psyche, the shift in experience produces an alteration in the paradigm and a significantly modified system of valuing and believing. The change does not change the inherent nature of the crystals in the kaleidoscope nor the inherent nature of personality dynamics. The person, gender, and mood may remain essentially the same in a human. But while everything is essentially the same, everything nevertheless is wholly different—seen in a different light, from a different perspective, forming a different sense of truth and reality.

Conversion

Christian conversion is a "significant emotional event." It involves a new personal relationship with God in Christ, a new insight regarding the truth about God and self, and a new trauma as one is confronted with an entirely new world of moral claim, ontological reality, and vocational destiny. Frequently Christian conversion involves all three kinds of events in conjunction. Sometimes the conversion starts in trauma, moral, physical, or psychical; and then moves through new insight to a new relationship. At other times it starts with a new relationship, often mediated through a new quality of human relationship, and moves on, therefore, to new insight and the new trauma of personality reintegration. At still other times it starts in new insights and grows to include the other two factors. Sometimes it takes place mainly on only one of the three levels.

In any case, Christian conversion is psychodynamically and sociodynamically like any other conversion and can be accounted for wholly as a significant event of the psyche, in terms of standard psychosocial models and Fowler's taxonomy of psychosocial growth. Humans are converted to Christianity and its faith experience from other faiths and/or from unbelief. Humans are converted from Christian faith to other faiths and/or to atheism. Humans are converted from hope to hopelessness, cynicism, or existentialist despair and vice versa. During the last two decades conversions in all of these directions have been nearly universal phenomena in the West. The crucial insight we must deal with is that all these shifts are the same dynamic phenomena. The key differences are differences in the content of the insight, relationship, or trauma. Sometimes the experience is of such a sort that the paradigm shift constitutes a new integration of the human personality in terms of God and his grace in Christ. That is Christian conversion, and we correctly speak of it as redemptive, since it can be demonstrated empirically that such conversion, when it is not distorted by psychopathology, frees, heals, renews, and embellishes human life. If on the other hand, it is Christian conversion but is so poorly worked out in a personality fraught with psychopathology, as we sometimes see in evangelicals, that it enlarges neurotic guilt and compulsivity, exaggerates anxiety and social alienation, and deepens narcissism and manipulative egotism, it is hardly Christian and surely not redemptive.

Other conversions can also be redemptive (from fascism to humanitarianism, for example) or sick (from benign American civil religion to obsessive dependency upon the arbitrary authority figures and structures of some cults, for example). The content of the conversion and the direction of the reintegration may be Christian, non-Christian, or anti-Christian. Any of the three may be healthy or sick, redemptive or destructive. Only that conversion, of course, can reintegrate a human personality to maximal redemptive consequence or wholeness, which does so in terms of God's grace, radical, unconditional, and universal. Such grace is the insight and relationship offered by the Judeo-Christian Scriptures. No other perception offers a reintegration perspective that is not based upon superficial "achievement worthiness" and "self-justification" strategies, ultimately self-defeating programs, spiritually, psychologically and socially, because of the negative motivation and dynamics they set in motion.

The critical point to be emphasized here, however, is this. What distinguishes one conversion from another is its content, not its dynamic. The process of all true conversions is a psychosocial process, accountable wholly in psychological and sociological terms.

This is a critical point for numerous reasons. First, it compels all humans to recognize that we take the position, perspective, or commitment we hold because of the initial faith assumptions that underlie our worldview or behavior. Second, it compels us to recognize that that perspective is held for psychodynamic reasons, not merely for rational, supernatural, theological, or cultural reasons. Third, it compels us all to acknowledge that the psychodynamics that impel us spiritually, as well as otherwise, form a growth continuum that we can condition in significant ways by the insights we seek, relationships to which we give ourselves, and the trauma to which we are willing to open ourselves without denial or repression. Fourth, it compels us to recognize that the growth continuum runs through a structured matrix of psychosocial growth stages, no matter what we do, which shape our destiny by the providence of God. Fifth, it compels us to insure that the content and conditions of that growth continuum, matrix, and process, in the lives of those for whom we have responsibility in home or clinic, are profoundly fraught with the good news and personal manifestation of God's healing grace. Sixth, it compels us to remember that when pathology appears in Christian life we must look for its sources in psychosocial factors. Seventh, it compels us to reject the supernaturalization of conversion, typical of some evangelicals, which is so self-defeating in its three implications: one, that spirituality is somewhat apart from and different than ordinary life; two, that the spiritual world is antipathetic to the natural world; three, that being God's people means being a little strange, culturally, socially, and spiritually. Eighth, it compels us to remember that God's world is one world and comprehends all processes together, that the whole process is natural not supernatural, and that his preferred modus operandi throughout history, in nature and in grace, has been to use the established dynamics of his natural processes for all things. Thus the taste of salt and its chemical reasons, the falling leaf and its gravitational guide, and the physics of snowflake crystals or the formation of coal are all supernatural in the same sense that the work of the Holy Spirit is supernatural. To put it another way, the work of the Holy Spirit, the phenomena of Christian conversion, and the dynamics of our transforming moments are no more supernatural than the formation of coal under the physicochemical laws of hydrocarbons under pressure. Only on that view will we have the motivation and the creativity to create the models for understanding what happens to people in conversion and, therefore, how to enhance that process of Christian growth to which the church keeps giving so much time and treasure so naively, and that psychologists continue to be so ignorant and ambivalent about. Ninth, it compels us to eradicate all remnants of suspicion about the authenticity or quality of each other's conversions, because they differ from our own in event or process.

Conclusion

Benedict J. Groeschel has provided an interesting model of spirituality conceived from the perspective of the contemplative monastic ideal.[9] He appreciates appropriately the essential psychodynamic drivers of spiritual growth. He notes that we move under the urges of anxiety on the one hand and the lust for peace and freedom on the other. We move through three phases (purgative, illuminative, and unitive) and on two levels (faith and life experience). He notes that the further we move toward the unitive phase of maturity—union with self and God in contemplation—the more we achieve peace and free-

9. Benedict J. Groeschel, *Spiritual Passages* (New York: Crossroad, 1983).

dom. Anxiety is progressively reduced. Clearly he is implying a reintegration of personality and personhood through a progressive
conversion process with the same essential dynamics as are indicated
above for the significant psychical event.

This is, I sense, also the primary manner in which Fowler sees conversion functioning within the structuralist paradigm. However, conversion to Christian faith and life is experienced in all manners and
forms imaginable. They range from the process of a general structuralist psychosocial development within the believing community to
sudden life-altering events.[10] All forms function in essentially the same
psychodynamic way with essentially the same psychosocial and spiritual consequences.

Fowler helps us to appreciate the ideal ultimate consequence of the
growth event or process of Christian conversion. True conversion leads
to the universalizing stage when we are able to embrace all in the joy
and freedom of realizing that all are embraced by God in his universal
grace and redemption.

10. Hugh T. Kerr and John M. Mulder, *Conversions* (Grand Rapids: Eerdmans,
1983).

10

Pastoral Counseling and Faith Development

THOMAS A. DROEGE

There have been relatively few attempts to relate pastoral counseling and faith development. Pastoral counseling has been linked historically to pastoral care. Faith development, fast becoming a separate discipline in theology, is generally linked to Christian education. Those alliances have been natural and appropriate, but it is time to bring these two unique theological perspectives into conversation with each other.

There are obvious similarities between pastoral counseling and faith development theory. Both are stepchildren of psychology and are suspect within some theological circles: They are stepchildren because their core concepts come from psychology; they are suspect because the language of both is more psychological than theological. Our discussion will show that some of the major differences between pastoral counseling and faith development have to do with psychological rather than theological issues. That is not to minimize the differences but only to point to a more fundamental problem that confronts both perspectives, namely, the justification of their theological identity.

Perhaps the most striking similarity between pastoral counseling and faith development theory is the importance of development to each. This is more obvious with the latter since development is at the very heart of its theory, but pastoral counseling has drawn heavily on

Sigmund Freud and Erik H. Erikson's theories of development along with Carl R. Rogers's growth metaphors. It makes almost no use of the structural theory of development of Jean Piaget, Lawrence Kohlberg, and James W. Fowler, while faith development makes only limited use of the life cycle theory of Erikson and Daniel J. Levinson, and virtually no use of Freud. This means that counselors often use development to define pathologies or sin, while faith development theory uses it to define healthy growth or sanctification. Evidence of this difference will be apparent in what follows.

There are three areas in which a dialogue between faith development theory and pastoral counseling seems most natural and appropriate: diagnosis, faith nurture, and transitions. First, both pastoral counseling and faith development theory have elaborate and sophisticated methods of diagnosis, though one probes pathology and the other growth. Diagnosis used to be a bad word among pastoral counselors, especially Rogerians, but Paul W. Pruyser and others have reclaimed the term for use within the perspective of pastoral care. Second, both pastoral counseling and faith development theory are concerned with the nurture of the whole person and ways in which that can be facilitated. Faith development theory focuses more specifically on the nurture of faith, a focus often lacking in pastoral counseling. Finally, there are resources in each theory for dealing with transitions and the crises that inevitably accompany transitions. Each focuses on a different set of transitions, one psychosocial and the other structural, but a dialogue on the similarities and differences can be productive.

The Theory of Faith Development

Developmental psychology has made great advances since the turn of the century, and the church has made direct use of its findings, especially in the area of educational methods and curriculum planning.

There are two broad traditions of developmental theory that have relevance for understanding faith. Life cycle theory, identified almost exclusively with Erikson for many years, provided an impetus to think about the life of Christians, including their faith, from cradle to grave. Recent studies in adult development have made life cycle theory an even richer resource for reflections on Christian life and faith. The other stream of developmental theory originated with the insights of Immanuel Kant regarding the a priori structures of the mind. It was Piaget who translated this philosophical insight into a developmental psychology of genetic epistemology. He describes a sequential series of increasingly complex structural stages in cognitive development. Kohlberg discerns a similar structural development in terms of moral judgments. Fowler uses a modified form of the same schema in distinguishing developmental stages of faith.[1]

These two approaches to understanding the developmental dimension of faith are complementary, the first psychosocial and the second cognitive. The life cycle approach identifies the existential issues of faith that are likely to be dominant at a particular stage of life; the cognitive approach shows how such faith seeks understanding through the capacities of knowing and valuing that develop in an orderly manner through a sequential progression of stages.

Development insights from the theories of Erikson and Piaget have only recently been applied to an understanding of faith. For centuries faith was described almost exclusively as an adult experience. The classical description of faith, dating back to Peter Lombard, is knowledge, assent, and trust. These three aspects of faith are ordered sequentially. Knowledge comes first, because it is necessary to know what is being promised or commanded before one can respond. Assent is the next step. It is considered an act of the will by which one affirms what one has heard and come to know as true. The final step is trust by which one clings to what has been promised. This classical description of faith makes sense for adults but not for children, especially those in the first years of life. One of the most divisive controversies in the early period of Reformation history was over infant baptism, which was really a controversy about whether children were capable of faith at an early age. On the basis of the classical definition of faith, they surely were not.

A developmental approach opens up a whole new way of understanding faith. For example, if trust is the foundation of faith as it is of the personality, as Erikson's theory would suggest, then it makes sense to hold up a little child, as Jesus did, as a shining example of faith. Then the educational task of parents and Sunday-school teachers is not to get some kind of content into children's heads (e.g., Jesus died for our sins), but to foster a felt sense of trust in the nurturing support of a holding environment.

Fowler has done more than anyone else to develop a systematic theory of faith development. Following the lead of Piaget and Kohlberg, he provides us with a schema of what I would call faith-knowing or faith seeking understanding. In "faith as knowing," the mind is actively engaged in forming the content of faith in patterns or mental structures. These patterns can and do change in predictable, developmental stages. On the basis of the empirical evidence of faith interviews, Fowler has been able to distinguish consistent patterns or stages

1. James W. Fowler, *Stages of Faith* (New York: Harper and Row, 1981).

of faith. Each of these stages has its place within a sequential order. The sequence of stages never varies. Furthermore, each new stage builds and incorporates into its more elaborate pattern the operations of the previous stage. This means that development from one stage to the next is always in the direction of greater complexity and flexibility.

Growth from one stage to the next is not automatic and not as directly related to age as are the stages in the life cycle theory. Biological maturation, chronological age, psychological development, and mental growth are all factors that affect the readiness to make a stage transition. Transitions occur when the stability of a given stage is weakened by crises, new disclosures, and challenges that stretch the person's present pattern of faith knowing.

The transitions between stages are critical junctures (crises) at which a person's life of faith can be severely threatened. A stage transition means a painful ending as well as a new beginning. It means giving up a total way of making sense of things. It frequently entails confusion, doubt, uncertainty, and what may appear to be a loss of faith.

Thus it is not surprising that people cling to one way of thinking even when this proves to be constricting and distorted. Fowler's research indicates that many people remain at the stage of conventional faith for an entire lifetime. It is important to remember that a particular pattern of thinking determines the stage of knowing in faith and not the content of the person's faith. People with widely different theological positions may share a common stage of knowing. At the same time two people who make the same biblical or doctrinal affirmation may employ two different ways of thinking about it.

Though this sketch of faith development theory is condensed and says nothing about individual stages of development, it should suffice as background for the dialogue that we wish now to pursue.

Diagnosis in Pastoral Counseling and Faith Development

One of the most obvious links between pastoral counseling and faith development theory is that each is concerned with diagnosis and each offers a conceptual apparatus for making a diagnosis. How important diagnosis is for pastoral counseling is a matter of continuing debate. Many pastoral counselors dislike the term *diagnosis* because they do not want to put labels on people, but in the broad sense of determining the nature of the problem, diagnosis has always been a part of counseling, including a part of the church's counseling. Faith stages are the diagnostic categories used in faith development theory. The Center for Faith Development Studies, which Fowler heads, has developed a rather sophisticated method of scoring faith interviews to determine the faith stage of particular individuals. Two fundamental issues need to be raised in relation to the diagnostic function of both pastoral counseling and faith development theory. The first has to do with the nature of the diagnostic categories: Are they theological, psychological, or a combination of both? The second issue has to do with the use of diagnosis in pastoral ministry.

In pastoral counseling the problem is primarily the fact that psychological rather than theological categories are used. As Pruyser observes in *The Minister as Diagnostician*, it is thought that the pastor's perspective should be theological, just as the psychotherapist's perspective should be psychological.[2]

The same critique can be made of faith development theory, which is heavily dependent on the developmental psychology of Piaget, Kohlberg, and Erikson. Fowler attempts to avoid that critique by making a sharp distinction between structure and content in his analysis of faith.[3] He maintains that the diagnostic categories that are used to discern faith stages show how faith works and not what faith says. Psychology helps us understand the structure of faith, and theology helps understand its content. It is not obvious, however, that structure and content can be that cleanly differentiated. To say that a person is in stage 2 rather than in stage 5 is to say something about the quality of his or her relationship to God and others, and not just something about the level of his or her psychological development.

As one who is trained in pastoral counseling, both AAPC and CPE, and who is immersed in faith development theory, I would like to offer a preliminary observation relative to this issue. I think that both pastoral counseling and faith development theory need to heed the warning of Pruyser. Pruyser's warning is not a fundamentalist call to ignore the insights of contemporary psychology but rather an insistence that the pastoral perspective on counseling and human development be unique and true to the faith of the church. I think Fowler heeds this warning more than the leading theorists of the pastoral counseling movement. He keeps the focus on faith and carefully distinguishes faith from other patterns of human development: cognitive, moral, life cycle. As Pruyser notes, pastoral counseling has not made a similar effort to differentiate a faith perspective.[4] He suggests the following categories in his own effort to distinguish a pastoral perspective: awareness of the holy, providence, grace, repentance, communion, and vocation. These categories may not be the best ones to define the pas-

2. Paul W. Pruyser, *The Minister as Diagnostician* (Philadelphia: Westminster, 1976).
3. Fowler, *Stages of Faith*, 99.
4. Pruyser, *The Minister as Diagnostician*.

toral perspective of faith, but I believe that such a perspective is needed in pastoral counseling.

Though Fowler is right in keeping the focus on faith, he defines faith so broadly as a human universal that the unique Christian meaning of the term is lost. The only place in his theory where a Christian emphasis shapes his description of the faith stages is in his use of the image of the kingdom of God to describe stage 6. Most of Fowler's critics argue that this is too much of a Christian focus. I think it is too little. A pastoral perspective needs a focus on faith that is uniquely Christian if it is to aid in a ministry to persons in their process of development. Let me cite one obvious example. A biblical study of faith reveals the centrality of trust for a Christian understanding of faith. In Fowler's theory trust is mentioned only in his description of undifferentiated faith, a description that is not even included in *Life Maps* and appears only as a pre-stage in *Stages of Faith*.[5] If pastors were to use Fowler's faith stages, their understanding of how faith works and of the kind of nurture it calls for would be deficient and their pastoral care and counseling would suffer.

I think that Pruyser is right when he says that the discipline of psychology can be used for theological purposes only after you have defined a *pastoral* perspective that is true to the Christian faith. My own constructive attempt to use developmental theory as an aid in understanding faith follows that methodology.[6] I use Erikson's life cycle theory as an aid in ordering the various elements or aspects of faith, such as trust, obedience, and commitment. I do not think it is advisable or even possible to make a sharp distinction between the content and structure of faith, as does Fowler, getting the content of faith from theology and the structure of faith from psychology. Scripture talks about the how as well as the what of faith when it refers to specific elements of faith like trust, obedience, commitment, and knowledge. A pastoral perspective on human development needs to be faithful to a biblical understanding of both the structure and the content of faith. A developmental theory can be used *within* such a perspective to aid in a ministry that is done *from* that perspective.

The second issue relative to diagnosis is a more technical one. It concerns the diagnostic categories used by both pastoral counseling and faith development theories. Generally speaking, pastoral counselors use psychodynamic categories and faith development theorists

5. James W. Fowler, *Life Maps: Conversations on the Journey of Faith* (Waco: Word, 1978); idem, *Stages of Faith*.
6. Thomas A. Droege, "A Developmental View of Faith," *Journal of Religion and Health* 3 (1974): 313–29; idem, *Self-Realization and Faith* (River Forest, Ill.: Lutheran Education Association, 1978).

use structural categories in making a diagnosis. The difference this makes for case analysis is brought out clearly by Carl D. Schneider in an essay on "Faith Development Theory and Pastoral Diagnosis." His essay was delivered originally to an annual meeting of the Institute for Faith Development sponsored by the Center for Faith Development Studies at Emory University. Schneider reports on a study that he and colleagues at the Pastoral Psychotherapy Institute did on a faith interview that Fowler included in *Stages of Faith*. This report is the only critique of faith development theory from the perspective of pastoral counseling of which I am aware. It is a valuable study, because it critiques Fowler's theory from within (i.e., the way it interprets case material with the aid of the diagnostic categories of stage theory).

> Fowler has the apparatus for a major advance in pastoral diagnosis. But his actual use of his instrument, in this case at least, is more a reversal of the classical Freudian position than an advance upon it. The classical Freudian interpretation of religious material was skewed toward a pathological interpretation, construed mainly in terms of its defensive function. Ego psychology has attempted to improve upon this formulation by reminding us that an adequate formulation would have to include both defensive and adaptive function. *But Fowler often seems to see only the adaptive function and neglects the defensive.*[7]

Schneider's thesis is that the structural categories of stage theory lend themselves to idealized and intellectualized interpretations. According to Schneider, Fowler's interpretation needs to be corrected by a psychodynamic perspective that is more sensitive to the defensive reactions of distortion and denial. Schneider uses Paul Ricoeur's phrase "a hermeneutic of suspicion" in order to analyze Mary's Pilgrimage, the extended case study in *Stages of Faith*. While Fowler classifies Mary as stage 3, Schneider suggests that she is stage 2 or at best is in transition between stages 2 and 3.

Though it is not feasible to report the details of his analysis, I find Schneider's critique convincing. He employs a different set of diagnostic categories, psychodynamic rather than structural, to interpret a deeper level of ego functioning that is more defensive than adaptive. Schneider does not argue for one level of interpretation and against another, but rather suggests that they can and should be complementary. His essay represents the kind of responsible conversation that needs to go on between pastoral counseling and faith development

7. Carl D. Schneider, "Faith Development and Pastoral Diagnosis," in *Faith Development and Fowler*, ed. Craig Dykstra and Sharon Parks (Birmingham, Ala.: Religious Education Press, 1986).

theorists. Though I do not know of anyone who has tried it, a structural theorist could make a similar critique of a psychodynamic interpretation of case material by highlighting the adaptive as over against the defensive function.

It is noteworthy that Schneider's critique is made from a psychological rather than a theological perspective. It is basically a difference between a Freudian and Piagetian point of view, though Schneider's ego psychology and Fowler's faith development theory have moved far beyond the founders of these two theoretical schemas of interpretation. The point to be highlighted is that the difference of interpretation between Fowler and Schneider is psychological and not theological. That does not make the difference trivial, but it does serve as one more example of what Pruyser has warned us about—that the pastoral perspective easily gets lost in a debate about different psychological opinions.

The Nurture of Faith

The diagnostic categories of pastoral counseling and faith development theory are useful only to the degree that they contribute to the nurture of faith. Both pastoral counseling and faith development theory are concerned about the nurture of faith. However, each has a unique emphasis that becomes sharper when compared to the emphasis of the other. Using the traditional categories to differentiate aspects of pastoral care (healing, guiding, sustaining, reconciling), the emphasis in pastoral counseling falls on healing and the emphasis in faith development falls on guiding. This difference is similar to the one that is made in relation to faith diagnosis, where pastoral counseling stresses cure and faith development stresses growth.

Seward Hiltner defines healing as "the restoration of functional wholeness that has been impaired as to direction and/or schedule."[8] For the most part, pastors as counselors will see themselves as healers. When making a sick call at the hospital they may see their role differently, for the physician is seen as a healer and the minister as a sustainer. That role differentiation matches the soul-body split, which until recently has been the accepted way of distinguishing between the functions of physician and pastor. But if pastoral counseling falls into the realm of the spiritual, then the pastor should function as a healer, and the role of healer is shared with mental-health professionals who have helped to define the nature of healing and wholeness.

Pastoral counseling begins with the assumption that there is an

8. Seward Hiltner, *Preface to Pastoral Theology* (Nashville: Abingdon, 1958), 90.

impairment, some problem to be resolved, some deficit to be removed. The function of diagnosis is to determine the nature of the predicament, but even if the predicament is not defined explicitly, both counselor and counselee have some sense of the functional wholeness that is the goal of the process. Counseling is a means of moving from the predicament to the goal.

This model of healing corresponds to the classic model of salvation. In the latter model, sin is the predicament, salvation is the goal, and being saved is the process of moving from one to the other. The healing model of pastoral counseling is at last analogous to the salvation model of theology. I would say that the former is a dimension of the latter, a part of the larger whole. This relationship has prompted Protestant ministers to be leaders in the pastoral counseling movement, including in the clinical pastoral education movement.

"What saves?" is a question that has always fascinated Protestants. The question assumes that the individual is in need of rescue, understood as some form of sinfulness. The saving power of grace, received through faith, enables the person to move toward the normative state of salvation or redemption. Theorists of pastoral counseling have changed the language: estrangement for sin, acceptance for grace, fully functioning for salvation; but the model is the same and healing/saving is the dominant concern.

Given this framework of understanding, it is not surprising that pastoral counseling theorists are critical of faith development theory for its failure to pay sufficient attention to pathology (sin). Again, Schneider's essay is an example. He contrasts Fowler's theory with Erickson's schema of psychosocial development, noting that Erikson identifies not only the task to be mastered at each stage: trust, autonomy, initiative; but also the result of failing to master the task: distrust, shame, doubt, guilt.

> Such polarities are absent from Fowler's theory. John McDargh, speaking of this tendency, suggests it may result from the influence on Fowler of the structural-developmental mode "with its characteristic avoidance of depth psychology's preoccupation with pathology. . . . This reluctance to describe faith in terms of a life trauma or inquiry that must be mastered seems to be the influence of the more ameliorative bent of structural developmental thought. . . .
> *The language of developmental fixation, immaturity, or repression is never evoked because of its presumed invidious connotations."*
> This is indeed a blind spot in Fowler's theory. When he turns to the difference between psychoanalytic and structural-developmental theories, the discussion tends to focus around the issue of the inability to *regress* stages in structural-developmental formulations. But even that

comparison is the most innocuous one possible. One talks merely of
going forward or backward, not of the possibilities of being warped,
bent, misshapen. Theologically, we might state this in terms of the *inadequate doctrine of evil and sin in Fowler's theory.*[9]

"What saves?" is not the only, or always the most important, question to be addressed by those who are charged with the responsibility
for nurturing faith. Faith is not only on the receiving end of a rescue
operation, but it grows and matures as an active expression of what
it means to be a Christian. "Justification by grace through faith" may
be the central core of a Protestant confession of faith, but a doctrine
of sanctification is necessary to describe the shape of the Christian life
both within the community of the faithful and in active involvement
in the life of the world. One of the major ecumenical contributions of
the Methodist tradition, under the influence of John Wesley, has been
to remind Protestantism of the importance of sanctification and the
perfection of faith. Faith development theory belongs in the center of
that tradition. It should not surprise us that Fowler is a Methodist and
that the Center for Faith Development Studies is located at Emory's
Candler School of Theology, a highly regarded center of theological
studies within the Methodist tradition.

The first thing one must say about faith is that it is the gift that is
rooted in and nourished by the forgiveness of sins. Having said that,
faith development theory becomes a marvelous resource for discerning
and facilitating the growth of faith to the point of its full maturity.

Guiding is the pastoral care function that best describes what will
emerge as central from a pastoral perspective shaped by faith development theory. Diagnosing the faith stage of an individual is useful if
it will aid in facilitating the growth of faith from one stage to another.
It is for this reason that Christian educators[10] have been much more
responsive to faith development theory than pastoral counselors. The
identification of structural stages of faith contributes directly to an
understanding of the concepts of intellectual growth and readiness for
learning that have always been at the heart of educational theory.

If pastoral counseling puts the emphasis on being saved, then faith
development theory puts the emphasis on the state or "way" of salvation. The stages of faith are clearly prescriptive as well as descriptive. Fowler acknowledges that "it has become clear that we are trying

9. Schneider, "Faith Development."
10. Thomas Groome, *Christian Religious Education* (New York: Harper and Row,
1980); Gabriel Moran, *Religious Educational Development* (Minneapolis: Winston, 1983);
John Westerhoff, *Will Our Children Have Faith?* (New York: Seabury, 1976).

to do both descriptive and normative work."[11] Each stage builds on and incorporates into its more elaborate pattern the operations of the previous stage. This means that development from one stage to the next is always in the direction of greater complexity and flexibility. It is for this reason that the more developed stages can be considered more adequate than the less developed stages. The structure of stage 5 is better than that of stage 3, though that does not mean that a stage-five person is better than a stage-three person or believes something different as far as content is concerned.

Can one be prescriptive about faith and the process of its development? That question points to what is most unique and also most problematic about faith development theory and about what it can tell us regarding the nurture of faith. Fowler is aware of the issue when he says:

> Perhaps most important among the developmentalists' contributions, and among the most controversial, are the visions they offer us of optimal human development. While claiming to be descriptive of human experience generally, developmental theories, overtly or covertly, point toward an end-point or fulfillment of the pilgrimage of growth, that represents a normative vision of the human calling and possibility. . . . The growing edge, in constituting developmental approaches to religious education, lies in the direction of reclaiming, in education and ethics, normative images of human excellence. These naturalistic accounts of human moral and faith development must be engaged by the necessity for conversion of the heart and will. Theology and developmental research are needed which can clarify for us the permanent modifications of the path of human development that result from conversion or justification, and from the resulting unfolding *synergy* of divine and human love. This means a renewal of attention to the process my theological forebear, John Wesley, called *sanctification*.[12]

In these words Fowler expresses the unique contribution of faith development theory, its emphasis on sanctification and optimal faith development, and its relationship to the process of justification by faith. Therein lies the difference between the two contexts within which pastoral counseling and faith development can and should be interpreted theologically. "What saves?" is the question that pastoral counselors ask. If taken seriously, it places one squarely into the doctrinal domain of justification. "How does faith grow?" is the question that developmentalists ask. If this question is taken seriously, then one is placed squarely in the doctrinal domain of sanctification.

11. Fowler, *Stages of Faith*, 199.
12. Ibid.

Ideally, the doctrines of justification and sanctification should be complementary. Practically, the tensions created by the different emphasis within each have been the cause of heated controversies. Is faith primarily a passive reception of a gift that comes from beyond the self or an active power within the individual that energizes and shapes the Christian life? Is faith primarily a mystery known only to God, or is it an empirical reality that can be measured and charted? Is faith a gift or an achievement? Is faith a human capacity and skill that can be strengthened and perfected or is it the power of God at work within us to do what we are not capable of doing? Are we to approach people with a hermeneutic of suspicion, never underestimating their capacity for deception and destruction, or do we look for constructive ways in which faith is working in the lives of people and attempt to nurture its growth?

The tensions between pastoral counseling and faith development theory may not appear in the form stated in the preceding paragraph, but I think the questions reflect the difference in theological orientation between them. The tension is a healthy one as long as these two ways of looking at faith are recognized as complementary. Each perspective is a partner in the dialogue about faith as a whole. The tension becomes destructive only when justification and sanctification become either/or alternatives for understanding and nurturing faith.

Periods of Transition

Both pastoral counseling and faith development theory have emphasized the importance of transitions: Pastoral counseling emphasizes the transitions related to situational crises such as divorce, bereavement, loss of job, and illness; faith development emphasizes the transitions related to the move from one stage to the next. Though there are differences between situational and developmental transitions, I want to focus on the characteristics that both have in common in order to highlight that they are times of high vulnerability and great potential for growth.

What is involved in transitions? First, they represent an ending. Most of us try to ignore endings by acting as if we can go through a transition without coming to terms with what is left behind. We focus on the challenges of the next stage, the next job, the next marriage. In teaching on a college campus, I witness each year the transition that every graduating senior must experience. I have sat through many commencement addresses but have never heard one that mentioned endings, much less one that used it as a theme. Yet for college graduates there are many treasured relationships that come to an end—

parting with friends with whom one has shared many intimacies, leaving mentors who have modeled a life of faith and hope, and departing from a community in which one's identity was shaped.

The second characteristic of transitions is that they carry people into a wilderness period, a time when nothing is firmly in place, a time when the pervasive feeling is a sense of loss. People are no longer who they were, and they are not yet who they will be. They are not sure who they are. Though this confusion is a normal and necessary part of a transition, it can be very unsettling, especially when there are no culturally established rituals to facilitate the movement between what was and what will be.

Only after we have attended to the first two characteristics dare we make the observation that transitions lead to a new beginning. Things fall into place, and the way into the future becomes clear. This does not happen all at once, and more often than not the new beginning is something that happens to a person rather than something the person chooses. Awareness of the new beginning may come as we realize that there is more order than chaos, more power to act than feelings of helplessness, more acceptance of self and world than self-doubt and self-contempt. As this happens, a surge of energy fortifies the person in transition for the new opportunities that make each new period of life and each new stage of faith exciting and challenging.

A transition is a painfully dislocating process of letting go and rebuilding. It means the dissolution of a way of being and knowing that was fairly stable and comfortable. It means living with ambiguity and a sense of uncertainty, often for a considerable period of time. It is no wonder that there is so much resistance to transitions, even when present modes of being and thinking prove constrictive and stunting.

In periods of situational or developmental crisis, then, there is often a need to go back to the roots of faith, back to trust as the sure foundation of faith. Both pastoral counseling and faith development literature describe the threat of chaos and the feelings of powerlessness that come to persons in transition. During such periods people often feel diminished and impoverished because there is so little to nourish a sense of self-worth and competence. The experience of people in transition is often like going back to the beginning of life in order to find a supporting environment and solid foundation on which to build a future.

It was Erikson who reminded us that trust is the foundation for both a healthy personality and faith. Or as he put it, religion supplies the systematic undergirding of basic trust for all of life. There is ample biblical support in both the Old and the New Testament for that insight. The supreme symbol of trust sustaining faith through a period of transition is the cross. All other transitions pale by comparison. Jesus was facing death, the most difficult of transitions, and the new beginning was not at all obvious. The crisis was magnified by Jesus' awareness of the importance of this event for the coming of the kingdom of God. He felt the awful pain of dislocation and abandonment in that wilderness experience. He was forsaken by almost all who had supported his mission, which now seemed a total failure. He even felt forsaken by God. Nevertheless, he called out, "My God, My God." In this call is the trust of faith in spite of a sense of being abandoned. It was this trust that sustained him as he approached his death.

It is this kind of trust that pastors need to nourish in people who are going through periods of transition. A careful reading of the pastoral care and faith development literature will sensitize pastors to such periods of transition and help them to identify the kind of transition that the person is experiencing. To recognize trust as the need of faith in such periods of transition can lead to an appropriate judgment about the kind of pastoral care that should be provided. At times the care may be nothing more than an attentive presence. At other times it might mean exploring values and beliefs. At yet other times it might be simply meeting material needs. Whatever form it takes, pastoral care makes real and concrete the promise of the gospel to which faith clings all of the time. One hopes this is especially true in periods of crisis.

Pastoral care has always responded in some form to the needs of people in transitions, but for the most part it has been an intuitive rather than an informed response. As a result, many transitions are understood poorly, or they are even resisted, by well-meaning pastors. It is a temptation for pastors to reinforce what Fowler calls a stage-three level of faith, a conventional faith that believes what the church believes. A transition to a more independent, critical stage-four level of faith is often painful. It is accompanied by doubts and often leaves the person isolated from the more conventional believer. For the pastor, it takes an act of courage to provide a supportive environment to a person engaged in such a transition, partly because the person may become a restless and disruptive influence in the community of faith. Nevertheless, the transition is vital to the person's life and to the life of the community of faith. Both pastoral counseling and faith development theory can provide us with reliable tools for facilitating this painful but productive process.

11

Faith and the Problem of Death

LYMAN T. LUNDEEN

Death touches all of us profoundly as both a fact and a threat. In the face of our hope for continued relationships and greater fulfillment, death comes to us as a stark end. We react to the possibility with grief, fear, anger, and confusion, even if it does not seem to lie in the immediate future. Whether it is down the road or will come with our next step, death challenges the very meaning of life.

Faith is a vital resource for those who face death. Trust in God's activity in Christ encourages both those who are dying and those who provide care for them. It lifts the spirits of the dying and frees the care-giver to extend honest, respectful support in critical moments.

Faith as a resource in care-giving has its spontaneous side. We do not have to think about faith for it to be active; typically we just bring our confidence in God with us into the sickroom. Nevertheless, it is helpful to reflect on the implications of faith for our pastoral approach to death. That is our primary task here. Specifically, I want to list and explore five proposals regarding the relationship between faith and death. The proposals are based on the assumption that faith affects the whole person and in turn is affected by the whole person. Consequently, what we think about the nature of God, the meaning of life, and the possibility of salvation impact on our experience of death and shape our efforts to minister to those who are dying. In this sense, faith and theology give direction to our caring. The clearer we are about our theological affirmations, the more helpful we may be in the face of death. In this hope, we turn to the first of the five proposals.

The Character of Death

Faith maintains the complex and mysterious character of death rather than provides a simple and universal solution to it.

Faith does not solve the problem of death but puts it in a living context of meaning. It reinforces the depth dimension of death, putting it in touch with the infinite. Faith then tends to expose the partial and projective character of all answers to death just as it confronts and enhances the wonder of one's human existence. Not only does this maintain the mystery of death but also it keeps us from reducing faith to mere superstition in which the joys of this life are too neatly projected onto some other world.

The popular notion of faith pictures it as bringing pat answers to the trauma of death, answers that focus on the survival of the individual and on some kind of compensation in another world for what we lose here. Whether such answers are patently religious or secularized hopes for peace and relief from struggle, their effects can be similar. Although we can reject these answers as being too simple or too arbitrary, the assumption continues to thrive that the claims of faith override the reality of death in a straightforward and final manner. Thus the end of life is softened so that it is not really an end at all. The individual is assured that he or she will live again, will face judgment, and if vindicated will find peace and happiness in another world. The resurrection and the last judgment are used as clear-cut supernatural answers to remove the sting of death and to give comfort to the survivors. In this way, the widely recognized Christian answers to death become part of the problem. By being used to oversimplify death and its consequences, they contribute to our repression of what actually occurs in death even as they are a distortion of the significance of faith. While much that is said in the Christian doctrines of resurrection and judgment can be affirmed, if they are used as too-simple solutions to the problem of death they are not very helpful.

When we try to bring the resources of faith to the deathbed, otherwise sensitive and caring people can let faith's answers close off deep discussion of feelings and circumstances. Elisabeth Kübler-Ross was amazed how many clergy felt comfortable "using a prayer book or a chapter out of the Bible as the sole communication between them and the patients, thus avoiding listening to their needs and being exposed to questions they might be unable or unwilling to answer."[1]

From the perspective of faith, it is important to recognize both the complexity of human experience and the diverse and partial character of our answers to it. Experience treated too simply loses the dimension of awe and wonder that is the soil on which faith must grow. And faith expressed oversimply becomes a kind of pablum on which it is difficult to sustain mature human life. If there is such a thing as the simple gospel, it is the simplicity of a living relationship to God and not the neatness and finality of any set of explanatory statements.

Faith helps us to see the ways in which death resists our attempts to understand and to deal with it. There are many facets to the death experience. Our problem is to keep any single way of looking at it from becoming so dominant that others cannot be perceived. For example, it is often assumed by both religious and irreligious people that death is something that is feared, especially if the person is not too old or too sick to enjoy life. An exclusive emphasis on the fear of death obscures other reactions to it, including what Sigmund Freud called the death wish. This point was brought home to me in a personal way. A clergy friend of mine had a heart attack and thought that death was imminent. While he was waiting for the ambulance, he had time to think about his impending departure. He had always anticipated that he would be afraid to die, that his family and friends would have such a hold on him that even faith would not sustain him in that moment. What he discovered was that he was not afraid at all. To his surprise, the only thing he thought about was all the committee meetings he would not have to go to!

The point is simple: Death is a unique experience for each person. We confront death through the medium of our own previous experience, and we color it with our own personal expectations. Thus death is different for each person. It belongs to a particular individual and occurs in a set of historical circumstances that are never duplicated exactly by anyone else. This is part of that mystery of death, and it invites us to consider new and surprising possibilities rather than trying to obtain exhaustive explanations.

The weight of personal expectations in understanding death makes death an opportune link with the concerns of faith. Death is always understood on the basis of vicarious experience: We see others die, and on this basis we develop our own hopes and fears about it. The old adage about there being no atheists on the battlefield is true, because when death must be faced honestly we are forced to anticipate it in

---

1. Elisabeth Kübler-Ross, *On Death and Dying* (New York: Macmillan, 1969), 226.

one way or another. At this point we realize that in respect to death human choices are decisive, especially the choice between faith and despair. We see that everyone of us interprets our existence in one framework or another, and on the battlefield it is more comforting to opt for the framework of faith.

The complexity of death as a human experience is articulated in the word *mystery*. Death can easily be thought of as a problem to be solved, almost like a mathematical equation. But death continues to be a mystery, and a mystery does not submit itself to exhaustive analysis or easy resolution. On the contrary, when a mystery is appreciated for what it is, the dimensions of depth and hiddenness often become more pronounced. In this sense, faith can help us see that death is not just another problem to be answered, not even if the answer is a religious one. It is more closely tied to the living fabric of each person's life than that. Thus death faced honestly and faith taken seriously keep us from a reductionism that makes death only one problem among many. By leading us to see how each person must deal with the meaning of life in the midst of the inexhaustible totality of things, faith protects the mystery surrounding human death. That mystery, even for faith, must be lived through, and not explained or believed away.

Just as death can be treated too simply, so the resources of faith have often been treated in a reductionist fashion. The emphasis has been on individual survival after death, compensatory satisfaction in another world, and fear of divine judgment that is often moralistic and mechanical. The disproportionate emphasis on the persistence of individual identity has often been translated into a popular piety where the soul has a natural immortality with each of us doing something to ensure our future habitation of heaven or hell. Careful attention to the biblical witness should have helped us to avoid this oversimplification. As death is a mystery, so the resources of faith have a diverse, open-ended, and unfinished character to them. This is ensured by the variety of interpretations given in Scripture and by the symbolic imagery in which Christian hope has always been couched.

Biblical views of death are more varied and more complementary than is often supposed. In many places death is seen as something to be feared, whether it is interpreted as the end of life or as the occasion for a final accounting before almighty God. In this perspective, death is the great enemy. It is the wages of sin, the punishment of a holy God. It can even be seen as a manifestation of the wrath of God, as his final opposition to the evil that has become entrenched in his creation.

A second scriptural view of death is the notion that death is a transition to a better life, a kind of final friend. It becomes significant as a gateway to a land of milk and honey where there are no more tears or sorrow. This view suggests that life is only a scene of frustration and tragedy and that death opens the door to fulfillment and victory with Christ. The apostle Paul talks about being eager to be with the Lord, but he also indicates that he is willing to stay here to do the work that is necessary. One of my seminary professors suggested that the class should be eager to have life end. I could not accept the idea, but it illustrates the notion that death can be an event anticipated in hope.

At least one other view of death in Scripture is important. It focuses on the way we live and die, and not on the discrete event of death itself. Death is seen as a symbol for an unfruitful and unfulfilling style of existence. In contrast, life (or eternal life if you prefer) stands for a meaningful and satisfying way of coping with circumstances. Both death and life then become symbols for the quality of our existence. They do not deny the Christian hope for the future, but they put the focus on the manner in which one is able to deal with present relationships.

In this perspective life and death are used in a metaphorical fashion. Given our preoccupation with facts and with literal descriptions, we might conclude that this approach to death is the most insignificant one in the Bible. In actuality, it might be the most profound. A symbol functions in the same way that faith must work if it is to prepare us for a difficult experience like death—it sets a direction and gives shape to our expectations. Or as Paul Tillich says: We need not think of symbols as "only symbols"; they are factors that shape experience and assist us in grappling with reality.[2]

Both the experience of death, then, and the answers of faith are more complex and more open to interpretation than they may appear. What we need in pastoral care to the dying is partial and useful claims rather than final and exhaustive solutions. Faith must offer more than pat assertions about life after death or escapist notions about satisfaction in another world. There are important promises in faith. A disproportionate emphasis on them not only contributes to the repression of death in our culture but also represents a radical distortion of faith itself.

Symbolic Resources of Faith

We have come to the threshold of a second proposal: Faith offers symbolic resources for dealing with death as a part of life.

The affirmations of faith are helpful in dealing with death not in

2. Paul Tillich, *The Dynamics of Faith* (New York: Harper and Row, 1957), 43, 45.

spite of their symbolic character but because of it. They are not primarily propositions about life in some other world. Instead they are images that provide a platform for dealing with the decisions facing us in *this* life. Deeply rooted in feeling and emotion, they convey power and courage that is not strictly dependent on their conceptual content. They arise in a community and therefore point beyond themselves to personal relationships in which our identity is established. Intellectually, they are partial and somewhat qualified in character. Only in this way can they avoid becoming idols that close us off from the living texture of life, both human and divine. In other words, they depend on the sustaining power of given relationships, not on some deterministic outcome of history that is miraculously predicted. They symbolize our hopes and expectations but do not themselves become the absolute guarantee of future fulfillment.

Assertions of religious faith can get in the way of an honest approach to life and death when their partial and symbolic character is ignored. For example, statements about resurrection and judgment can become so final in their purported authority that they tend to repress reactions to a grief situation. In a similar fashion, the will of God or the naturalness of death can be used to soften the sharpness of death. Expressions of doubt, anger against God, or even a sense of intense loss may seem inappropriate in the face of firm and final faith claims. One hopes the symbols of faith can be held in a way that encourages honesty and freedom rather than thwarts them. Anger, humor, and doubt are protective and creative human reactions to all profound experiences, including death. Surely they should not be repressed in the name of faith!

A similar point is made by a story of a dying clergyman who did not think the expression of anger against God was appropriate. With a sense of humor and flexibility, a wise counselor said to the patient, "Don't worry, God can take it!" This kind of openness to human emotion ought to be encouraged rather than discouraged by faith.

Tillich opts for openness in faith from a slightly different angle.[3] He claims that contrary to popular opinion, faith and doubt are not mutually exclusive but are compatible with each other. To have faith is not to believe without doubt but to have confidence even when doubt and criticism are allowed to surface in all their power. This means that faith is more than knowing things that others do not or believing things that others cannot. It is the willing acceptance of not knowing, of not being certain of everything that is affirmed.

At the time of death, the most basic contribution of faith may be

3. Ibid., 101.

this combination of trust and agnosticism that is able to leave the future in God's hands without the demand for a detailed road map or a precise religious warranty. Being supported by human and divine relationships, a person may be able to use the symbols of faith and not repress his or her honest reactions to impending death. The symbols of faith also mean that we care-givers have no excuse for turning away from people who are dying. The resources of faith throw us back into the concrete situation of immediate responsibility. The symbols of hope point to the future, but because they do so in a partial and incomplete fashion they leave us with the need and the opportunity to deal with the present. In any case, people who are dying need to receive the symbolic resources of the faith again and again. We cannot offer them once and then leave dying people to their own resources.

To recognize the symbolic nature of our religious affirmations does not make them less effective in our circumstances. The symbols of faith reflect our particular identity in a historical context, bringing out all the unique and nonrational facets of our actual existence. They cannot be reduced merely to literal attempts to describe what is easily expressed. Instead, as Tillich would say, they are no less than symbols, contributing to our most fundamental grasp of reality.

It is not new, of course, to recognize the symbolic character of the claims of faith. Theologians have long recognized that the fulfillment of faith's promises must be pictured in metaphors that stretch the imagination to its very limits. The New Testament writers demonstrate the vivid images to which God's love leads. But in a time when astronauts are probing space and there is not room for pie in the sky, there is a real need to be honest about the symbolic character of religious answers. The conditions of finite history make symbols both necessary and useful, but it is always important to strive for some modesty in our expression of the details of Christian hope.

Emphasis on the symbols of faith has an added benefit. It alerts us to the dependence of terminally ill patients on odd and indirect ways of talking about their own death. Perhaps sensitivity to the symbolic ways we talk about life on both sides of the grave is very important.

As the care-giver speaks and offers gentle indications of the hope that God's love generates, the dying and the grieving may be freed to tell their own stories of both hope and fear. Experiences out of the past may surface in ways that require careful sensitivity to their symbolic function. The end result of sharing on this image level may well be the cultivation of sustaining interpretations of this one death in terms that can be genuinely appropriated by those who face such threat of loss most directly. Just so, the resources of faith in God are free to do their own work.

Faith Recognizes the Tragedy of Death

This brings us to a third proposal: Because the Christian faith affirms the importance of finite history and the individuals who participate in it, it encourages us to take the specific circumstances of each person's death seriously.

The thrust of faith drives us toward contemporary priorities and experiences as a basis for an assault on the future. In giving us resources for coping with death, faith points us to existing relationships, including the presence of God. All our talk about an afterlife is based on the importance of special experiences in this life. It is not, as it is so often construed, a denial of the significance of this world and of the particulars that constitute history. In other words, faith is not so much heavenly fire insurance as a way of coping with the hard decisions that go into facing death. It helps us deal with death as a part of life. The framework that it provides supports us in the death situation only if it offers us a perspective that is capable of giving us an orientation for the rest of life, no matter how brief that may seem to be.

Christian hope, then, is a claim about the resources that are available to people in the context and the flux of finite experience. It builds on the capacity of historical relationships to sustain us throughout the adventure of life. It gives people a central place and priority but not in opposition to community. It asserts the dignity of each human being in the face of natural circumstances and human responses that all too easily deny that dignity. Faith encourages us to involve ourselves more fully in the uniqueness of our own presence with others. It is in that context that hope and courage must prevail. Romans 8:31ff., which is often used at funerals, proclaims that nothing can separate us from the love of God. This proclamation is not primarily a statement about some distant future but about a present relationship that cannot be broken. In this sense, even this statement of faith turns our attention toward present encounters rather than away from them,

Looked at in this way, faith makes each person's death more important than we might assume. It reinforces the sense of grief and loss instead of short-circuiting it. It hurls us back to attend to the dying and grief-stricken individuals with our presence and care. When the individual is the proper object of *our* love and the surprising object of God's concern, then death becomes even more tragic and faith stands forth in its real power. This may be one of faith's finest contributions—to enable us to see the full tragedy of human death instead of accepting is as natural or as an easy route to heavenly bliss. Helmut Thielicke, a German theologian, puts it this way: "Death becomes a much more serious matter the more we have to lose, that is, the more we are aware of the true destiny to which we have been called, the more we know of the dignity and uniqueness of our person, which death strikes down."[4]

Faith helps us to deal with the actuality of death by introducing the same resources that are helpful in other circumstances of life. Those resources turn on a concern for others and reflect the possibility for creative and courageous action in the worst of circumstances. They come from the Christ event and its audacious claim that divinely given resources are effective in our historical relationships. These resources give love and hope in the face of pain and imminent loss. Because a pastoral presence communicates this hope, it can help people die more faithfully. It lets love shine through in the midst of grief, not by denying loss but by standing with the mourners on their way through it.

The claim of faith is that Christ can sustain not only in the heat of battle but also in the ongoing struggle with the unknown, the tragic, and the unpredictable. Faith is not confidence in a split-level mansion in heaven but a confidence in the one who faces death with us in the same way that he has helped us face life. It orders our priorities and gives a meaning for life in the face of death, where life is seen as the opportunity to shape our relationships even as we depend upon them. The occasion of death then is a time to be there with those who face it. Confronting death together is the fruit of faith in the One who loves without letting go. Any faith that calls us away from that adventure, which is the historical struggle for justice and love, must be questioned both in respect to its truth and in regard to its biblical base.

Faith Enables Love at Difficult Times

A fourth aspect of the relationship between faith and death can now be elucidated: Faith suggests that we should be alert to present experiences of grace that can free us to love with courage even in a crisis.

If there is a God who is involved in our lives, we must know something of him now. All future hope rests on the fact that a given experience of life's meaning is continually tested in our history. We should look carefully at the religious dimension of all experience and be attentive to the possibility that we can be in touch with the Lord of history now. God is either available to us in the mundane affairs of life, or he is irrelevant to us in a crisis like death.

Too often the emphasis of faith on a future life detracts from what

4. Helmut Thielicke, *Death and Life*, trans. Edward H. Schroeder (Philadelphia: Fortress, 1970), xxiv.

we require in this life and from the signs of hope that enable us to face the future. The basic confirmation of faith is to be found in what is happening now. The living Christ meets us in the flux of our finite circumstances in such a way as to give shape to all our present priorities and expectations. If that is not so, any extrapolation toward the future can hardly be persuasive. It is from the vitality and content of this relationship that we gain a confidence in the belief that death is not the end. We are sure that this life is not merely subject to the whim of circumstance but has a place in God's purpose. In other words, the weight of confirmation falls on what is given now, not on what will be available in some remote future. The claim is that the relationship with Christ, which is given in and through our finite circumstances, is so impressive and persistent that it generates and maintains confidence in the belief that our personal relationships cannot end in nothingness. The basic experience of life's meaning on this side of the grave generates whatever hope we have for eternity. Pastoral care contributes to that experience by calling to mind relationships of church and family. It brings the word of God in incarnate form. It has itself the power to reflect the present care of God. Then confidence in facing death can be primarily in the God who brings life out of loss, both now and in the future.

In its confrontation with death, then, the witness of faith points again to life. It alerts us to what may be available in this life to sustain us in the face of our apparent end. We are driven to focus not only on the predictive truth of religious claims but also on their present capacity to point us to available resources for human freedom and fulfillment. Paul, in his famous citation of theological virtues, gives priority to neither faith nor hope, the two virtues that are most strongly oriented toward the future. Instead, he gives primary emphasis to love, to that present experience that is indeed the ground of faith and the basis of hope.

Resurrection as a Symbol

On the basis of our preceding discussion, we come to a final proposal: The doctrine of the resurrection should be broad enough to give shape to our entire life as well as to sustain our hope and courage at the time of death. This proposal focuses on the doctrine of the resurrection, but similar comments could be made about the other symbols of faith that are related to death and dying.

Resurrection of the body is a symbol, arising out of a situation in which mystery is persistent and where some sort of symbolic framework is required by life. It affirms both the ultimate importance of finite individuals and the effective presence of God's liberating power in human relationships. It is a claim about living that includes an approach to death as one event in our history.

The resurrection as a symbol alerts us to the possibility that life comes from death in a most surprising manner. Every set of circumstances is the death of some opportunities and the emergence of others. Every moment is a time of new beginnings empowered by God's gracious love, which flows into our life through the lives of others. We are therefore free from being dominated in our situation by the power of circumstances. Thus the resurrection becomes a lever for social and personal transformation, because it affirms the novel possibilities inherent in every context. We need not be defeated by any threat, not even by death.

The resurrection as a symbol also establishes the importance of finite circumstances as the arena in which the fundamental drama of history is developed. While they need not control or defeat us, those circumstances call for our best creative response to the new possibilities that God holds before us. To love to the point of dying, even when it is our own death, may be the greatest test of faith. So the resurrection as a symbol of faith asserts both our freedom from the control of circumstances and the possibility of acting for good within them. It becomes a symbol with very practical effects, coming into play on the deathbed even as it has informed a whole style of life. It frees us for innovation. It releases us to love each other in the midst of rejection and loss. It enables us to cope creatively with death as one more adventure in life. It can help us to die well, celebrating human relationships even on the occasion of their historical conclusion. To put it in a word, the resurrection symbolizes a way for people to live and die.

Conclusion

We have considered several possible ways in which the relationship between faith and death can be seen. They deserve further consideration, but for now we will only point to the example of Dietrich Bonhoeffer, pastor and theologian, who in his own way has encouraged us to reflect carefully on life and death. Bonhoeffer's life was an affirmation of unexpected possibilities. Even in his death he could see his execution as a new possibility in the love of a God who had sustained him in all the struggles of life. As he was taken to the scaffold, he is reported to have said, "This is the end. For me the beginning of life."[5]

5. Dietrich Bonhoeffer, *Letters and Papers from Prison*, trans. Reginald H. Fuller (New York: Macmillan, 1953), 14.

Bonhoeffer witnesses to the confidence symbolized in the resurrection. He manifests a style of expectation that builds on the experience of God's grace and looks to the surprises that God has in store in every circumstance. He gives no neat explanation of the problem of death. Instead he invites us to be more sensitive, honest, and creative in the circumstances that are given. At the end of life he makes life itself an adventure that cannot be closed off, not even by death.

12

The Family as a Context for Change and as a Changing Context:
A Sign That God Is Always Making Something New

HERBERT ANDERSON

The Family and Change

The family is an organism of change. Individuals within a family change as they grow up and grow older. The needs of the family also change as a consequence of change in membership and circumstances. Other changes are less anticipated but equally disruptive. In order to remain a context that fosters individual growth, the family must also be able to adapt to change. The family is never a fixed sum. It is always in the process of becoming something new. Adaptability is therefore an essential characteristic of a family's capacity to move toward a future in which God is always making something new. To believe in a living God is to recognize change at the center of faith and life and the family.

The structures of the family are also altered in response to changing needs and circumstances in relation to society. The family has survived as a unit in society because it has been adaptable to changing social and economic needs. Because the family as a structure in creation is always in the process of becoming something new, it is neither possible nor desirable that its form remain static. Because God is still creating, nothing that lives is finished or complete. To believe in a living God is to recognize change as an inevitable characteristic of family structure.[1]

This affirmation of the necessity of change can be unsettling. It seems to be the opposite of stability. Like individuals, families seek to establish stability by limiting change. Our conviction that God is always making something new is covered over by our fear of change. Sometimes that fear prompts families to establish fixed patterns of interaction that limit a family's capacity to adapt. Families for whom change has generated more grief than they can endure frequently restrict the development of their children in order not to experience more loss.[2]

None of us is capable of tolerating infinite change. The trauma of change and loss is softened by continuity in the world we can observe. The complexity and diversity of creation and its changing character are balanced by the continuity inherent in the natural order. Families seek to establish this continuity in the midst of change through customs, traditions, rituals, the preservation of heirlooms, the naming of children, the fostering of family myths. Although each of these may solidify a family's future in continuity with its past, that continuity may be at the expense of the freedom of individuals within a family to maximize their gifts.

Because we are likely to err on the side of continuity at the expense of human freedom, we need to be reminded that change and continuity coexist in the being of God. We are to anticipate change in creation because the same God who orders the becoming of all things insures their continuity in his being. The observable forms of continuity that we establish in life and in the family are signs of continuity in the God who makes all things new.

We have assumed for some time that individuals change according to relatively predictable phases. Each phase is marked by a crisis that needs to be resolved in the interest of individual growth. It is now generally understood that the developmental process extends through the entire life cycle. People change and grow from birth to death.[3] As

1. Herbert Anderson, *The Family and Pastoral Care* (Philadelphia: Fortress, 1984), 33–40.

2. Norman Paul, "The Use of Empathy in the Resolution of Grief," *Perspectives in Biology and Medicine* (Autumn 1967): 161.

3. Erik H. Erikson, *Identity and the Life Cycle* (New York: International Universities Press, 1959).

a consequence the family must also be thought of as the context that encourages the growth of adults as well as children.

This shift has made it even more imperative that each family achieve a balance between the needs of the community and the needs of the system. The family as a structure must have enough cohesiveness and adaptability to endure the stress produced by the growth and change of its individual members. Every individual life-cyle crisis is also a family crisis. Individual transitions into and out of different family roles—such as leaving home, getting married, becoming parents, coping with widowhood—are all interrelated with changes in the family as a system. The family's capacity to change will create a context of freedom for individuals to grow.

The changes that occur in a family's history can be marked by five epochs. The family as a social system changes according to its own history of changing tasks. Each of these epochs is identified by a predictable crisis of change in response to which the family must adapt in ways that will continue both individual growth and communal accessibility. What is distinctive about this proposal is that the five epochs are not only determined by individual developmental tasks but by the needs of the family as a whole. This approach does not diminish the importance of individual developmental agendas. It rather shifts the focus to the family as the social unit that is responsible for creating the kind of emotional space that will maximize the growth of each of its members.

Such an emphasis on the family's life cycle also provides a useful introduction to understanding the family systemically. Because the family has a life of its own that is greater than the sum of its parts, one can also say that the family qua family has its own history. I agree with Murray Bowen's suggestion that a life-cycle format may provide "one of the most practical and effective ways to help people find a quicker understanding of the family as a unit."[4] Pastoral ministry to individuals experiencing a life-cycle crisis is also ministry to a family system that itself is in a crisis requiring adaptation and change.

Family Ritual: Transitions of Change

A family's adaptability to change is frequently sustained by the development of rituals. In this sense, a family ritual mediates between individual and communal needs. It is a symbolic process that unites or otherwise influences its participants to act in a way that supports

4. Elizabeth A. Carter and Monica McGoldrick, eds., *The Family Life Cycle: A Framework for Family Therapy* (New York: Gardner, 1980), preface.

the organism as a whole while at the same time allows for individual development. Family rituals are also a way of mediating between continuity and change. They form a bridge between the past and the future. We keep traditions alive in order to maintain continuity with our history. If those traditions become paramount, however, there is increased likelihood that the system will remain closed to its environment and to change as well. People do not serve traditions; for the family, as for any human community, traditions exist to serve people.

A ritual is an action, or series of actions, sometimes accompanied by formulae, that regulates transactional patterns within a family. A ritual may be overtly prescribed in terms of time, place, and participants. For example, in connection with a family reunion or birthday celebration, it may be fully spelled out who is to come, what they are to bring, and how long they will stay. A ritual may also be more covert. Family routines like putting children to bed or eating a meal usually evolve in a less explicit way.[5]

The way a family navigates through difficult moments in its life cycle is frequently enhanced by rituals. Some of those rituals are shaped by cultural custom; others reflect contemporary social patterning; still others are formed by the sacramental structures of a religious tradition that may also be culturally linked. Family rituals help to keep the family's story alive and available for succeeding generations. Family rituals also mediate between individual and communal needs in order to foster intimacy appropriate to a family's life-cycle task. Human systems need rituals that structure accessibility in order that gracious moments of intimacy may happen.

Rituals provide necessary structures of transition that balance individual development and family change. Families may have ceremonies surrounding the start of school, the beginning of menstruation, the receiving of a promotion, the recognition of achievement, or leaving home. Every major event of an individual's life is a family affair. Rituals are one way by which the family as a system can adjust to the changes that will be occurring in its life. Families that function best will never allow the system's needs for stability to disrupt the individuating moment for one of its members. Rituals that work best will honor autonomy and celebrate community simultaneously.

Family History and Pastoral Intervention

Understanding the family life cycle provides the pastor with a framework for thinking about how ordinary pastoral interventions

5. Anderson, *The Family and Pastoral Care*, 98–105.

around the church's ritual life correspond to critical moments of transition in the family's history. In each of the five epochs in the family's history there are rituals in the church's life that correspond to the family's principal task. Pastoral work is enhanced by these ritual moments. They provide structured access to people in families at those times of transition when the system is likely to get stuck. Pastoral ministry often requires delicate balance between attending to individual needs and attending to the needs of the family as a system.

The dialectic between individual and community is embodied in the ritual life of the church. On the one hand, the rituals of the church focus on incorporation into community: we are baptized into the whole company of the faithful; the eucharist is a community meal; marriage makes "one flesh" of two separate individuals. Although our communities change and enlarge, they are never eliminated: the Christian is forever understood as part of a people. On the other hand, rituals of the church are also moments that foster individuation. Throughout the Christian's life, each of us is identified as a distinct and unique child of God. The Christian life, even at rituals of transition that intersect with the family's life cycle, is always both individual and corporate. Understood in this way, the rituals of the church can undergird the family's task of helping people learn how to be together separately. Similarly, the rituals of the family that maintain this same dialetic between separateness and togetherness also make it possible for people to claim their uniqueness as a gift from God for service in the world.

One of the distinct privileges of pastoral ministry is its access to people in crisis. Sometimes those crises are unexpected and traumatic; other times they are expected and potentially traumatic. The literature in pastoral care has primarily examined unexpected crises in human life such as death or sickness or divorce. Since the developmental process has been extended to include adulthood, more attention has been given to the pastoral care of individuals in expected crises throughout life.[6] The introduction of a family life cycle adds yet another perspective to this approach to pastoral care. Ministry to individuals experiencing a life-cycle crisis is also a ministry to a family that is in a crisis requiring adaptation and change. Our ministry to families is at the same time a focus on individuals in the midst of community.

In each of the following five epochs, I have identified family tasks, a dialectic that shapes those tasks, impediments to the achievement of those family tasks, and pastoral opportunities to assist families in

6. Donald Capps, *Life Cycle Theory and Pastoral Care* (Philadelphia: Fortress, 1983).

living through those epochs in ways that enhance both individual growth in autonomy and communal stability. It should be noted at the outset that this is a normative approach to the family life cycle. For that reason I have not attempted to examine the consequence of divorce for this schemata.

The Family Life Cycle: Five Epochs

Epoch 1: Forming the Family

Tasks. The process of leaving father and mother in order to form a new family requires shifts in loyalty and role identity that are never easy. The central task of this first epoch is to establish clear but permeable boundaries between the newly forming family and each family of origin in order that the process of marital bonding may occur with a minimum of either fusion or confusion. The process of emotional bonding or joining the marriage depends on satisfactory differentiation of self from one's family of origin. And so the biblical admonition is correct: you must leave before you can cleave (Gen. 2:24). Premarital pastoral work with couples is more effective when the focus is on leaving home and clarifying the boundaries of the newly forming family system.[7]

Although in some families the wedding is the primary ritual for leaving home, the process of differentiation of self ordinarily begins early in life and continues long after marriage. Some families make it easy for children to leave; others set up major roadblocks along the way. In other family situations, it is the children rather than the parents who are unwilling to sever their emotional connections to their families of origin.[8]

The goal of this life-long process of differentiation is self-definition. It has to do with developing autonomy, becoming free to differ, valuing one's worth, and claiming the validity of thoughts, feelings, wishes, and fantasies because they are one's own. It means that one's body is one's own—to cherish, nourish, and use responsibly. Being individuated is a prerequisite for interdependence and emotional bonding for community.

Even if the process of differentiation and leaving home has gone well from the beginning, getting married is a significant and some-

7. Kenneth Mitchell and Herbert Anderson, "You Must Leave Before You Can Cleave: A Family Systems Approach to Premarital Pastoral Work," *Pastoral Psychology* 30 (Winter 1981).

8. Howard M. Halpern, *Cutting Loose: An Adult Guide to Dealing with Your Parents* (New York: Simon and Schuster, 1976).

times traumatic moment in the process. If, however, the wedding is *the* leaving-home ritual, it is not surprising that all the events surrounding the marriage ceremony are so highly charged. The process of "joining the marriage" depends on emotional separation from one's family of origin.[9] Each partner in marriage needs to be sufficiently free of other loyalties in order to make a commitment to the other and to the task of becoming married. That process of bonding is enhanced by the complementarity of needs met, physical intimacy, emotional affection. More than that, however, the process of bonding is an intentional act of mutual commitment in which a husband and wife honor the uniqueness of each in the covenant bond of marriage.

Dialectic.   Learning how to be together separately in the family is the central dialectic that must be internalized by the family system in this first epoch. The family that provides a stable context for growth and change is governed by a balance between intimacy and distance, between being together and being separate, between being close and being distant, between individuation and participation. Augustus Napier and Carl Whitiker have said it well:

> We feel that the family's capacity to be intimate and caring and their capacity to be separate and divergent increase in careful synchrony. . . . The more forceful and independent they become, the easier it is to risk being intimate and close. The more closeness, the easier it is to risk independence.[10]

This dialectic is fundamental for effective family functioning. It is essential in order to establish boundaries within a newly forming family system that are both clear and permeable. Too much togetherness makes for unclear boundaries within a family; too much separateness diminishes the accessibility that is possible when boundaries are permeable. Too much closeness does not give each family member sufficient freedom to discover all the gifts he or she has to give to the world. Too much distance undercuts the kind of community stability that is essential for growth to occur. Individuals can grow only in participation with other fully developed selves. Individuation and participation are equally necessary. Being separate together is not something added to human life; it is something essential for life in communities and families.

9. Salvador Minuchin, *Families and Family Therapy* (Cambridge: Harvard University Press, 1974), 16–45.
10. Augustus Napier and Carl Whitiker, *The Family Crucible* (New York: Harper and Row, 1978), 93.

Impediments.   If one thinks about all the roadblocks in the way of getting married, it is amazing that marriages last as long as they do. The following list begins to identify what might impede the processes of leaving and cleaving that are necessary for forming a family.

Parents who do not let go and children who will not leave maintain loyalties to their families of origin that create unclear boundaries in a marriage; this in turn impairs bonding.

The extended adolescence that is prompted by economic dependence related to a lengthy process of education complicates leaving home.

For those who have lived singly for some time before marriage, there are both alliances and life patterns that are difficult to relinquish for the sake of marriage.

Early pregnancy thrusts a newly married couple into the parenting role and diverts attention and energy from marital bonding.

Preoccupation with work or study on the part of one or both marital partners generally does not allow for either enough time or energy to work at joining the marriage.

The process of leaving and cleaving is central in the epoch of forming the family. Both facets of the process take time and work and often considerable risk. One of the goals of pastoral ministry during this epoch might be to structure occasions that will encourage work on these tasks in a supportive context.

Pastoral opportunities.   Pastoral work with couples prior to marriage is an opportunity to assist them in continuing the task of leaving father and mother. There will be time ahead for focus on the bonding begun during courtship. Anyway, people about to marry are enough in love or in heat or both to keep the connection going—if it is sufficiently freed from the emotional claims of family of origin. For this reason, we have proposed that premarital pastoral work should do the following: clarify each individual's relationship to his or her family of origin; encourage the process of differentiating oneself from one's family of origin; and enable the couple to see clearly and as a whole the most important features of their relationship to each other.[11] We have found little resistance in looking at families of origin in order to explore the legacy each is bringing to the formation of a new family.

Both individuals have expectations for marriage based on what they

11. Mitchell and Anderson, "You Must Leave."

have experienced and observed in the families that raised them. What is most beneficial in premarital pastoral work is to help people discover the stories, motifs, and attitudes that have shaped their expectations. This may be done in a couples' group or with one couple. The genogram is a useful and nonthreatening way to begin the exploration. In some ways it resembles a family tree. What is different about a genogram is the stress on stories and traditions of emotional ties that go beyond mere facts. One should look for distance and closeness in family relationships, how naming may be a way of handing down a special blessing, particular roles and rules and rituals that help to maintain the family system, and traditions that each partner is eager to hold on to or discard in forming a new family. Robert F. Stahmann and William J. Hiebert have identified a similar purpose: "In the family-of-origin exploration, our purpose is not only to look at and trace the parental models which a man and a woman bring into their relationship, but also to trace how these models influence their own behavior and with each other."[12]

Premarital work that has as its focus the encouragement of people to leave home and to be, at the same time, aware of the great power of the patterns learned in the family of origin, is the kind of care that is most helpful in establishing a good marriage. Pastors may use a variety of techniques to accomplish the same goal. But the techniques are not as important as the attitudes with which pastors approach couples. If, as pastors, we can see behind every couple about to be married a host of other family members dancing that family's particular dance, and if we understand that the dance steps each bride and groom know best are the steps they learned to tread in their families of origin, we may have a more profound influence on that bride and groom than if we and they are trapped into the false assumption that they are only marrying each other.

It is important that the wedding ritual embody the dialectic of leaving and cleaving. Parents (not simply fathers) symbolize their letting go by the blessings they give as a part of the marriage ceremony. It is equally important that children about to marry ritualize their leaving father and mother in addition to the pledges they make to one another. The way in which the wedding ritual (and its preparations) proceed will deter or enhance the couples' tasks of leaving and cleaving.

In contrast to most other helping professionals, pastors have an opportunity to take initiative with people when they anticipate critical moments in the family's life cycle. Six months after the wedding is

---

12. Robert F. Stahmann and William J. Hiebert, *Premarital Counseling* (Lexington, Mass.: Heath, 1980), 71.

one such time. Some pastors have built into the marriage covenant a marital check-up after a designated period of time. Providing an occasion (perhaps in a group context) to examine the ups and downs of early marriage is one way that pastoral care can work toward the prevention of irreconcilable crises later in the marriage.

Epoch 2: Enlarging the Family

Tasks.   The principal task of the second epoch is to make space and time in the family for the addition and nurturance of children in order to insure the future of generations. The family is ordinarily enlarged through the birth and adoption of children. Whereas the task of the first epoch is to establish a structure that honors autonomy and celebrates community, the task of the second epoch reflects the family's procreative purpose. Having and rearing children in the context of a family is the way humans in all times and places have cared for the future.

From the Christian perspective, the having and rearing of children is itself an expression of faith, hope, and love. It is both a gift of God and a service to the human community. When we say that children are a gift, that affirmation is grounded in the conviction that children are one way that God continues to care for creation. The procreation and nurturance of children is a reminder that the family does not exist for its own sake but in order to participate in God's ongoing creative activity.

Procreation cannot be understood apart from a child's right to good parenting. The obligation to nurture the young is mandated by creation as surely as the necessity to procreate. In order to insure adequate nurture, the environment into which children are born needs to be a secure and welcoming space. The nurture of children, particularly during this epoch of enlarging the family, requires that parents be willing to sacrifice their own desires and aspirations in order to attend to their children's needs.

Fulfilling the procreative task requires a role change that does not automatically occur with the birth of children. For a variety of reasons, the role of parent may not be readily assumed by those who are biological fathers and mothers. The system must change as well. Patterns of interaction within a family are fundamentally altered whenever a new person is added. The capacity of a family to make these changes will in large measure determine whether it becomes a safe environment for nurture and growth.

Dialectic.   If the procreative task includes nurture, then from the beginning of life patterns of interaction and family attitudes are in support of the development of autonomy in the midst of community.

The dialectic that informs this second epoch is an attitudinal one. Parents need to be "crazy about their kids" while at the same time remaining aware that their children are not their children. Adoring parents make it possible to overlook soft spinach on the television screen and fill up the child's primary need for narcissism. The absence of such adulation at the beginning of human life is likely to lead to an impoverished sense of self in adulthood.

Children are a gift and not a possession. From the beginning, it is essential that parents remember that their children are not their children because they belong to God. That is another way of encouraging individuation. There is no room in families of Christians for close-binding parent-child relationships that restrict individual growth. Children are regarded as separate persons from the start. Because our children belong to God, it is our responsibility to help them become separate and distinct beings who are nonetheless committed to participation in meaningful community. Individuation is neccessary for Christian vocation.[13]

Impediments. The kind of environment that the marital pair has begun to create during the first epoch is crucial for the addition of children. Ideally it is an environment that has space for children. Unsatisfactory resolution of the primary family task may create a family environment in which there is no space for children or one in which children are expected to fill a vacuum.

  Biological fathers and mothers who have not differentiated sufficiently from their families of origin have difficulty accepting the responsibility of parenthood because they would still rather be children.

  Parents who have not let their children go tend to undercut their adult children's fragile parenting confidence, generally with the best interest of their grandchildren in mind.

  Mothers and fathers who are preoccupied with self-fulfillment at work or play may not be able to make space available in their lives for children.

  Parents who are overinvested in parenting frequently expect children to fill a vacuum created by unrealized dreams or the loss of a significant relationship.

  For those couples whose bond was more like fusion than intimacy, the birth of a child may threaten marital closeness with new demands for intimacy.

13. Anderson, *The Family and Pastoral Care*, 59–68.

> For couples who are more distant than close, an unstable triangle
> may be formed in order that the child provide the needs for close-
> ness in one or both parents.

> Competition for affection among siblings or between a parent and
> a child intensifies the possibility of conflict and fixed alliances
> that produce rigid rather than permeable boundaries.

Pastoral opportunities.   The two ordinary contacts that a pastor has
with parents at the time of birth are opportunities to reinforce each
side of the central dialectic of this epoch. The pastoral visit to the
hospital is ordinarily a time to celebrate the absolute uniqueness of
new life. Each child is viewed by his or her parents as the most beautiful ever born, even if the nose resembles grandfather's. The pastor
joins the praise and thereby participates in a process that fills the child's
narcissistic needs. When the birth is in any sense problematic, it is
more difficult but equally important for the pastor to help parents
celebrate the gift of new life even as they grieve the loss of the child
of their dreams.

The second opportunity for ministry is at the occasion of baptism
or dedication. Pastors are more and more inclined to take seriously
the importance of pastoral visits around this ritual event. Part of the
purpose of those visits is educational in order to reinforce the significance of the ritual of baptism or dedication. Pastoral visitation around
this ritual event is also an occasion to discuss the new addition with
parents and other family members. The birth of each child is a family
crisis. Discussion about how the child's name was selected or how the
sponsors were chosen will usually reveal important agendas for family
conversation. Most of all, a pastoral visit around baptism or dedication
is an opportunity to remind parents that they are caretakers and not
possessors of the child. Baptism or dedication of the child contributes
to the development of human autonomy, because it is a reminder to
parents to let their children go so that they might become autonomous
enough to serve the world for Christ's sake. Our children are not our
children even when we love them as our own.

There are educational opportunities within congregational life that
may assist parents through this delicate task of having and rearing
children. Support groups and classes for young parents within a parish
context are a splendid resource so long as they do not undercut the
parents' very fragile sense of competence. Family activities in the
church should provide ongoing support for family tasks.

Epoch 3: Expanding the Family

Tasks.   It is not surprising that the third epoch is a turbulent time
for families. It is a period of significant change for both children and

parents. Even the most stable families are affected by the rapid changes that occur during adolescence. During this epoch, parents are beginning to experience the crisis of middle years. While youth are trying out their options before a basically unclustered landscape, middle-age adults are increasingly aware of finitude and a diminishing horizon.

For parents and children alike it is a time of self-discovery. Therefore the task of the family during this epoch is to create enough openness in the system so that there is freedom for each individual to discover his or her distinctively separate and worthwhile self. Within the family, that must include openness to the diversity that is the result of fostering individuation. In relation to the outside environment, the family needs to be marked by mutuality, interdependence, and the easy exchange of people and ideas between the system and its environment.

This principle of openness for the family is a theological mandate. The family must be a open system if it is to foster in its young a sense of moral obligation to a larger ecology. Because the creation is an open system in which God's creative activity continues to make all things new, being a closed system is contrary to the eschatological vision in which finite systems are open to God's new creations. The privatization of the family is not just the harbinger of moral bankruptcy; it violates God's intention of an open and interdependent creation.[14]

A family characterized by openness is able to adapt to change initiated from within the system or from outside because change is recognized as normal and even desirable to enhance the self-worth of its members. Communication patterns are clear, rules are flexible, and roles are interchangeable.[15] And yet an open system is not without boundaries or ways of distinguishing between individuals or units within the family and between a particular family and its environment. The family as a human system, like the whole of creation, is an ecosystem of separate parts interrelated in a wonderfully mysterious and complex way.

Dialectic. The dialectic of this epoch is another variant of the theme of being separate together. It is a time when we are keenly aware how commitment to the whole enhances each part and the recognition of each part enriches the whole. In other words, interdependence within family systems and between the family and its environment is a delicate balance between autonomy and mutuality. We promote community by honoring the uniqueness of each individual. Having the

14. Ibid., 41–49.
15. Virginia M. Satir, *Peoplemaking* (Palo Alto, Calif: Science and Behavior, 1972), 112–19.

courage to be as a part *and* as the whole are inextricably bound together. The more clearly communal our anthropology is, the easier it is to encourage individuality.

Impediments. It should be clear by now that the unsatisfactory resolution of each preceding task will itself impair the family's functioning in subsequent epochs. The establishment of clear and permeable boundaries in the first epoch is essential if a family is to develop the kind of openness necessary for the third epoch.

Families in which the rules are rigid and covert are not likely to provide the necessary freedom for continued growth in autonomy.

Families that have not learned how to contain the conflict that results from diversity may severely limit both individuation and a free exchange with the environment.

The family that turns inward and seeks to become an emotional refuge from the world is not likely to endure because it has lost its purpose and its ability to transcend itself.

If a family's relationship to its environment is too open, then it is possible for the system to be overwhelmed by excessive stimulation and more diversity than it can reasonably integrate.

Pastoral opportunities. Participation in first communion, which in most Christian traditions occurs around the beginning of this third epoch, is primarily a communal ritual. The eucharist is a community meal. Participation in that meal of the family of God is the ritual that constantly reaffirms the belonging to one another that characterizes those who have been baptized into Christ. Regular eucharistic participation from as early age as seems appropriate strengthens the baptized child's sense of belonging to the people of God. For the sake of family stability during this epoch, ritual participation in the meal of the family of God is a useful reminder of the necessity of community.

The rite of confirmation or believer's baptism emphasizes the second part of the dialectic of this epoch. It is the recognition that each individual is a single one accountable to God and responsible to his or her Christian community. The religious ritual at puberty is a critical moment in the formation of identity and autonomy. The child-becoming-adult needs to be responded to in many communities as a person whose gradual growth and sometimes radical transformation make sense to those who begin to make sense to him or her. Religious rituals at puberty are essential as yet another instance in which individual autonomy is fostered for participation in ever larger communities.

It is most likely during this period that a pastor will be asked to respond to a family that will identify an adolescent as trouble. In some instances, the adolescent may be troubled with intrapsychic developmental issues or struggles with peer relationships. It is more common, however, that the family as a whole is troubled and has simply selected the most obviously troubled (the adolescent scapegoat) to divert attention away from the family. The first and most important help that a pastor might give such a family is to help them identify the problem as a *family* affair and seek the appropriate help.

Epoch 4: Extending the Family

Tasks.   The openness to include new ideas and patterns during the third epoch is a precursor to the task of the fourth epoch. During this time, children leave home and new members may be added to the family by marriage. The family's task is to extend its boundaries to include that new membership and a wider vision of the universe of belonging. A particular family is understood to be where its members are. It may extend from Phoenix, Arizona, to Hibbing, Minnesota, to Durham, England, to Lagos, Nigeria.

New membership in the family, whenever it occurs, always brings about change. The family circle of our childhood is but an arc in the family circle of adulthood. Whatever images we have as children or parents of small children of the family as a stable, narrow, and permanent thing changes during this epoch. Holiday gatherings often symbolize those changes. The group of people connected by blood or by choice that gathers at Thanksgiving extends the family, adding leaves to the table, stretching as far as the turkey and time allow.

As our families change, as they merge and marry and mate with others, we also learn something about the undercurrents and connections that join people. Each family is a sign of the extension of human community that ultimately reaches around the world. Such extension parallels the call of Christian discipleship that pushes us out of our narrow nurturing communities into ever-enlarging circles of interaction and concern in which God continues to make all things new.

Dialectic.   The dialectic of this epoch requires of parents what the first epoch requires of their children. In order to maximize the freedom for children to leave home and thereby extend the family, parents need to believe that loving their children means letting them go. Only if parents let them go are their children free to return.

Our understanding of love is often dominated by images of embrace or holding. Holding a child in one's arms is a universal picture of care. An embrace is an equally common sign of intimacy between friends and lovers. To be held by another is comforting and nurturing and encouraging and affectionate and sensual. Experiences of being held are essential for the survival of infants and necessary for bonding and care throughout life. Emotional connectedness, as well as physical touch, is an inescapable dimension of human experience. We all need to be held.

This need to be held by those we love and by those who love us is distorted when it becomes holding on that is possessive and restricting. What is a sign of life at one point in human development becomes a symbol of death at another stage in the life cycle. Sometimes families will go to extreme lengths to keep their children stuck in the family. Separation is perceived by parents as abandonment. "Parents cleverly avoid being abandoned by teaching their children to be helpless, fearful and dependent. . . . Children learn to protect their parents from feeling abandoned by never being capable enough to leave home."[16]

From the beginning of human life we are eager to test our autonomy, exercise our freedom, move toward that which is new and inviting. Holding and letting go are parallel dynamics in the developmental process. While the image of holding predominates during the epoch of enlarging the family, letting go is central for the fourth epoch. Although our need to be held never ends, this epoch is one of those times when we particularly need to hold one another without holding on.

The inclination to hold on is not limited to parents and children. It is particularly critical that husbands not hang on to wives in any way that restricts their growth. Some women have responded with drastic action to the feeling of being held down by husbands who were fearful of letting go. On the other hand, it has not been easy for women to take bold steps in the interest of their own growth because they have been accustomed to the protection of confinement.

This epoch is a time of letting go of emotional attachments as well as physical bonds. The family is being radically changed by the addition of new members. Distinctions between "us" and "them" diminish, even in our view of the world. We also need to let go of dreams of ourselves and for our children. We hang on to what we love as well as who we love with less tenacity.

Impediments.   Because this is the epoch when children ordinarily leave home, the changes *seem* more dramatic than at other times in the family's history. It is therefore an epoch when efforts at adaptation may be mixed with nostalgia and attempts to minimize change.

16. Sonya Rhodes with Josleen Wilson, *Surviving Family Life: The Seven Crises of Living Together* (New York: Putnam, 1981), 199.

If the self-understanding of parents is heavily dependent on the parenting role, it is difficult to let children go.

Parents who have been overinvolved in the lives of their children may attempt to continue that overinvolvement even after children have left.

In this epoch, as well as the next one, parents who have not attended to their marital relationship may discover they are strangers in an empty nest.

Menopause and other midlife changes can exacerbate or be exacerbated by the changes in the family constellation.

The care of aging parents may become a new preoccupation for middle-aged children who are reluctant to give up the parent role.

In this epoch, and the next, the death of one or both parents is added to the grief for children leaving home.

Pastoral opportunities.   The ministry to parents around the time of a wedding is a forgotten pastoral task. For the sake of both parents and children about to marry, I believe that it would be helpful to include both sets of parents in a premarital conversation focused on discovering family traditions. The marriage of children is indeed a time for celebration but it is also a time for grieving. It is a time for sadness. It takes courage as well as love to let children go. A part of pastoral ministry with families in the midst of change is to name the loss and encourage grieving.

The death of parents of middle-aged sons and daughters is generally more traumatic than we acknowledge.[17] For some adult children, the death of a parent is the occasion for autonomy at last. When the last parent dies, there is also a sense that the buffer against death is gone and we are next in line. Some parents have provided the emotional stability that enables families to hang together. Pastoral initiative with adult children when their parents die is important. It may be the first self-conscious experience of letting go.

Epoch 5: Re-forming the Family

Tasks.   The first task of this final epoch in the family's history is for the marital pair to reestablish their relationship without primary preoccupation with parenting tasks. Letting children go is sad but it is also liberating. It is an opportunity for couples to renew a personal

17. Herbert Anderson, "The Death of a Parent: Its Impact on Middle-Aged Sons and Daughters," *Pastoral Psychology* 28 (Spring 1980).

and intimate life together. How well this re-forming task is accomplished will depend on the quality of bonding in the earliest stages of family life, the extent to which couples have attended to their relationship even while bonding was primary, and their willingness to work at creating a new intimacy.

For some couples, facing one another without children as intervening buffers is a frightening prospect. Their major shared interest has been their children. Without them, husbands and wives discover that the emotional distance between them has fostered indifference and boredom. Re-forming the family requires that the marital pair recapture some lost parts of their relationship, let some patterns go, and discover new ways of being together. This new intimacy in the parent dyad creates freedom for everyone in the family.

During this epoch, the family is also re-formed as the older generation ages and passes away and a new generation is born. Grandparents, parents, and children all learn to reconnect in new ways. The normal crisis of aging usually increases the intensity of relationships between generations. Parents become grandparents at the same time they must care for their own parents. The early or unexpected death of either parents or a spouse is a crisis for everyone in the system. Re-forming the family is a continuous process that creates space for new marital pairs to begin the cycle again.

There is considerable overlap between the tasks of the fourth and fifth epochs. Because children are marrying later, the task of welcoming new membership occurs later in the family's history as well. The re-forming of the marital dyad may therefore precede the task of extending the family. In any event, letting children go is privotal. It is easier for children to form their own families if they leave home with a blessing.

Dialectic.   The balance between being separate and being together that has dominated each of the previous epochs is equally necessary in re-forming the family. The intimacy of the parental dyad makes it easier for children to leave home in ways that allow them to come home again. Relationships between grandparents, parents, and children are regularly an interplay of intimacy and distance.

Re-forming the family is also a process caught between remembering the past and anticipating the future. Husbands and wives who need to rebuild a marital relationship after the parenting tasks are over can neither ignore the past nor be bound by it. Even the best marital relationships will need to expect something new in the epoch of re-forming. There is also an increased sense that it is important to preserve the remembrances of the elder generation that is passing away. It is equally important to recognize that children who are leaving home will create their own family traditions and values. For everyone in the family it is a time of generativity in which the preservation of the past and the anticipation of a new future are in tension.

Impediments. Because this final epoch in a family's history may cover at least half the length of a marital relationship, many changes may occur. Families that have not learned how to grieve will seek to minimize loss-producing change in order to diminish grief. Moreover, within every family the life tasks of the elderly interact with the concerns that are prominent for child and grandchild generations. Intergenerational conflicts that arise may vary depending on the relative ages and concurrent stages of family members.[18]

- The distance created by the absence of attention to the marital relationship may be an unbreachable chasm.
- Overattention to the needs of a parent of middle-aged sons and daughters may divert energy away from the task of re-forming the family.
- Children who do not leave or who leave and come back home again may impede parents from re-forming the marital bond.
- If both husband and wife are involved in demanding careers, the time and energy left for one or both may not be enough for the task of re-forming the marital bond.
- Families that are overwhelmed by consecutive deaths have difficulty devoting energy to the re-forming of the family that those losses necessitate.

Pastoral opportunities. Perhaps the most common event of pastoral access with families in this epoch is to be present at the celebration of a wedding anniversary. Some couples have used the occasion of their twenty-fifth wedding anniversary to reaffirm their wedding vows. The marriage of children, the death of parents, and the retirement of one or both spouses are times of family crisis during this epoch when pastoral initiative would be beneficial.

Conclusion

I have attempted to outline some of the changes that can be expected to occur as a family moves through its history. Each epoch has

18. Carter and McGoldrick, eds., *The Family Life Cycle*, 210.

certain predictable tasks that must be accomplished in order that the family remain a context of growth for each member. There are other crises that are less predictable. Moreover, families have often established rules or patterns for coping with change that impede growth. In that sense the sins of mothers and fathers are passed on to children of the third and fourth generations. We leave to our children and their children our own unsolved problems with our parents. "Staying connected to—and at the same time separate from—our families parallels the life long struggle to create intimate/independent relationships throughout our lives. Balancing intimacy and individuality is a major theme of surviving family life."[19] By making the most of the cycle of family crises, we participate in the future that God is always making new.

19. Rhodes, *Surviving Family Life*, 275.

13

Pastoral Care and Social Change

LeRoy Aden

Christians are commanded to follow the example of Christ by caring for each other. "This is my commandment, that you love one another as I have loved you" (John 15:12). "Bear one another's burdens, and so fulfil the law of Christ" (Gal. 6:2).

The mandate to care comes in a world of change where we are confronted constantly by new and threatening developments. The world is changing and expanding in many different ways—by space exploration, by technological advances, and by new and undigested discoveries. I do not want to minimize the importance of these changes, but neither do I want to dwell on them. I am more interested in the upheavals that are occurring in our personal and interpersonal worlds—upheavals like the changing patterns of marriage and families, the friction between the sexes, the tension between the races, the many minute ways in which our social worlds are not the same as they once were.

Confronted by these changes, our tendency is to back away and, instead of caring for each other, to hold onto our own secure worlds. Yet we are challenged to care. That challenge seems to be reinforced in a circuitous way by the humanistic expectations that operate in our contemporary cultural milieu. We live in an age of expected self-actualization, basking in the hope of personal fulfillment. Not only do we think that we *should* be healed of all infirmities but also we tend to believe that we *can* be.

One of the obvious extensions of this outlook is the belief that we ought to be malleable, like a lump of clay. We ought to be able to change and be open to new developments without much stress, and certainly without any despair. Our experience tells us otherwise. We observe that we have a tendency to shrink, to close up in the face of a changing, expanding world. That observation brings us to our first task—the task of determining the level at which we are threatened by significant change. Our discussion will show what we confront when we are commanded to care in a world of social turmoil. In a more positive vein, it will help us to move beyond monological accusations toward honest dialogue about mutual concerns.

The Threat of Change

Paul Tillich helps us to clarify the nature and intensity of the threat. He does so in his analysis of the human situation as set forth in *The Courage to Be.*[1]

Tillich deals with our self-affirmation, with the ontological fact that we affirm ourselves as living creatures. He maintains that self-affirmation is always threatened by nonbeing, by forces that threaten to destroy us. This threat creates anxiety—not just fear but a basic and unbearable apprehension at the center of our existence. For Tillich, anxiety takes three different forms according to the three ways in which we affirm and assert ourselves. Any of the three forms can cause us to pull back, to shrink from the world. It is my hunch that the changes that we are experiencing in our lifetime threaten us on all three levels.

First, there is moral anxiety. According to Tillich, we are not only given life but also are asked what we have made of it. We are accountable for the gift, for life is not just given to us but it is also demanded of us. We ask of ourselves: "What have I made of life?" And the answer always comes back, "Less than I should have," for we lose our destiny and go against our essential self. This failure threatens us with moral anxiety, absolutely in the form of condemnation; relatively in the form of guilt. On a clinical level—or should I say on a personal level—we experience moral anxiety as a sense of guilt or, more faithfully, as a sense of shame.

Moral anxiety is increased when there is someone reminding us of our failures. Since we do not live and relate as we ought, it is good and necessary that we see ourselves in the mirror of someone else's

1. Paul Tillich, *The Courage to Be* (New Haven: Yale University Press, 1952).

evaluation. And so the increase of moral anxiety, of guilt, is not bad in itself, but it alone will not prompt us to change. It may only paralyze us. For those of us who have big superegos already, it only increases the sense of guilt to the point where we focus on the guilt and forget the issue. For others it increases the drive toward perfection, either by denying all moral obligations and trying to appear innocent or by rigidly following all moral demands and appearing to be the paragon of goodness. And these reactions are certainly aggravated when the one who accuses stands over against us in a self-righteous way, implying that the problem is ours and ours alone. We can see through that facade, or if we are unable, we can at least resist it in the name of our own need to be on the right side.

Second in Tillich's scheme of things is spiritual anxiety. He sees us as centered creatures, and he maintains that we must be centered in a reality beyond ourselves. We must participate in and be a part of a world beyond our own private world. We participate, not necessarily by creating something new and creative as a genius does, but by belonging to our cultural context and by making our own particular and significant contribution to it. Tillich calls this participation "spiritual self-affirmation." He extends it to our relationship with God and maintains that we must be centered in a meaning that gives meaning to all meanings. This means, in any ultimate sense, that for life to be meaningful, we must be centered in God.

The loss of this meaningful participation, on whatever level, threatens nonbeing. It creates spiritual anxiety, the dread of not having, the sense of not belonging. It takes the relative form of emptiness; the absolute form of meaninglessness.

On a clinical or personal level, spiritual anxiety is usually experienced as depression, ranging all the way from simply feeling blue to a morbid desire to get rid of the self.

If we have no resources to bear spiritual anxiety, we retreat from the world and paint ouselves into a corner. Underneath we are driven toward false certitude. We are tempted to eliminate the element of doubt and meaninglessness in our lives by building a narrow castle of absolute truth. "This is the way it is, and I will not allow it to be otherwise." With this declaration we turn our backs on a changing world and live in a world of fabricated and narrow truth. A prison-like existence, Tillich calls it.

Finally, there is ontic anxiety—the threat of nonbeing to our very existence. This anxiety is absolute in terms of death, relative in terms of fate. Fate does not refer, as we usually think, to the fact that we are subject to causal determination, to a world of pushes and pulls. Instead fate refers to the fact that we are contingent creatures, that our lives have no ultimate necessity.

Behind fate stands the absolute threat of death. Or as Tillich says, "The anxiety of death overshadows all concrete anxieties."[2] Thus a change in a world that we have carefully built up is not just an incidental happening. It may represent a deeper change, a threat to our very existence. Or a change in the status of various groups in the community, for whatever reason, may not just be a change in the way we relate to them. It may represent the death of a world and therefore in some sense *my* death. I am not saying, of course, that therefore we should have no change. I am only asking that we recognize that change induces ontic anxiety.

If we cannot tolerate ontic anxiety (and who can?), we are driven to take steps against it. According to Tillich, we strive for security—the kind of security in which the limitations of life, the truths we do not want to see, are shut out. It allows us to live in a manageable world, even though it is a false and inhibiting one. It allows us to muffle the fact that we are contingent creatures, that our way is not the absolute way. It is essential, of course, that we hear the message, but ontic anxiety tends to close our ears to it.

As Tillich sees it, then, there are three forms of anxiety. Any one form is sufficient to shut us down. If we are threatened on all three levels (e.g., by someone who implies that we are guilty, that our world no longer exists, and that we are dispensable), then indeed we are confronted by a threat that would prompt us to fight for our lives, either openly or in secret. The question "How can we be empowered to care in the midst of change?" is even more cogent, especially since the Christian faith will not let us retreat. I propose that we consider the challenge to care in the light of our morality.

Death and the Challenge to Care

In recent years there have been persons or groups who have tried to challenge us to care by inducing guilt or by assigning blame. That procedure will not work, especially if it is promoted in a we/they context. It only increases anxiety and covers up the duplicity of those who are pointing the finger.

Contemporary pastoral care has come up with another suggestion. It says that we should listen seriously and intelligently to the story of the other person and by listening help him or her to become more open and more loving. That is not a bad answer—in some sense it hits the heart of the matter—even though it has been repeated so often that it tends to become trite.

2. Ibid., 43.

Our Tillichian analysis indicates that love alone will not do it. The challenge is more difficult and demands something more radical. Tillich implies that in order to care we must acknowledge and come to terms with nonbeing. In my terms, we must begin to face death, to see our life in the context of its limits rather than to continue to deny our mortality.

By facing death, I do not mean death as an abstract possibility but death as a personal, existential fact. Nor do I mean that we should become morbid about it or obsessed with it. Instead I mean living with the fact that we are finite, limited creatures whose lives have undeniable boundaries.

Facing death, of course, is no automatic cure for what ails us. But, as a recent article in the *Christian Century*[3] notes, death can be an effective teacher of wisdom. Its lessons can help to promote dialogue in the present situation. In fact, I think the lessons are in some sense essential to caring for each other in the midst of social change. There are four lessons that I want to discuss.

First, death puts our lives and our pursuits in proper perspective. It not only prompts us to evaluate our life but also provides us with a criterion for judging the value and significance of many of our endeavors. To realize that someday I will die adds a perspective to our vision that exposes the triviality, indeed the egocentricity, that is often implicit in our concerns and aspirations. In this sense, death frees us from transient preoccupations and helps us to focus on more enduring ends.

In terms of a changing world, death relativizes our cherished values. It puts in proper perspective our treasured positions over against the tendency to absolutize them. Thus it allows us to see truth on the other side by reminding us that our formulations are not absolute ones, that the issues that we are so concerned about need to be put in a larger framework—above all in a framework that is concerned about the welfare of the community over against the pursuit of our own autonomous or egocentric ends.

The first lesson can be put in a related way: Before death all of us are equal. Status and power do not count. No matter how rich or poor, significant or insignificant, we all fall before death.

When our particular style of life is threatened and we feel anxious, the first thing we tend to do is to construct distinctions. We elevate ourselves, or our own particular group, and believe that we are more potent, and more life-giving, than all others. Ernest Becker, in *The*

3. Marcus Borg, "Death as the Teacher of Wisdom," *The Christian Century* (Feb. 26, 1986): 203–6.

Denial of Death, elaborates the tendency in great detail.[4] He maintains that we cannot stand our creatureliness, our finiteness, and that as a result we strive for immortality, attempting to be of infinite significance in our own particular world.

Becker rightfully exposes the truth that death, or at least our fear of it, prompts us to inflate ourselves inordinately. What he does not acknowledge is that death, faced honestly, can be a great antidote to self-inflation. It reminds us that we are all subject to extinction and that in death we are neither absolute nor eternal.

In this sense, death can serve as a handmaiden of the gospel, showing us that before God there is neither Jew nor Greek (Rom. 10:12). At the very least, death—to the extent that we own it as a fact of our existence—drives us toward humility, and by driving us toward humility, it drives us toward each other in care. It changes the terms of our relating to each other. Instead of seeing relationships in terms of power, of death-denying tactics, we see ourselves and the other person as persons in need, as equals before issues that are larger than our own self-inflated ones.

To take this lesson seriously is to encourage dialogue with each other where there are differences. We have had precious little dialogue. Instead we have had accusations, one group standing over against the other, applying labels to each other to cover up our own anxiety or bigotry. Before death we may become more dialogic, knowing that all of us are moving toward the same fate, that in some deep sense we are all much more human than anything else.

The second lesson of death is that it confronts us with the end point of our own self-seeking. We pursue our own ends, and end up by losing life and ourselves. Or in Eberhard Jungel's words, we drive toward relationlessness, alienating ourselves from God, the source of life, and isolating ourselves from each other by the pretense of self-sufficiency. In the process we die! Physical death is only the final expression of our estrangement, our relationlessness.

On a clinical or personal level, death to many of us means falling out of relationships. We dread the approach of death because it means becoming isolated and cut off from people around us, not just as we go down into death but from the very moment that our loved ones discover that we are terminally ill. We become unwanted reminders of mortality in a society that is obsessed with death's denial, and thus we are pushed into a corner where we are forced to deal with our plight all alone.

On the positive side, awareness of death prompts us to reexamine

4. Ernest Becker, *The Denial of Death* (New York: Free Press, 1973).

our relationship with others. It urges us to take advantage of the time we have together by making those relationships more honest and satisfying. It can move us to care, not just for those who are close to us but also for those with whom we share a common humanity. Self-inflation of any kind, or against any group, ends in the loss of oneself. In a word, it ends in death. In this sense, the awareness of death can cut through our self-seeking and prompt us to seek fulfillment in and through others.

Death teaches a third lesson: It shows us that there are no easy solutions to our situation. In Reinhold Niebuhr's fine phrase, redemption is not a simple possibility. Thus death corrects our contemporary tendency to assume that healing and fulfillment are easily achieved. We cannot master death; we do not even domesticate it very well. Thus it stands as a stubborn reminder that life is ambiguous at best and that the transformation of human interactions is difficult all along the way. That fact does not mean that we settle for the status quo or give up the necessity to change. It does mean that we must patiently support each other in the face of anxiety.

It also influences the nature and intent of our pastoral caring. Contemporary pastoral counseling, having bought into the promise of achievable self-actualization, puts heavy emphasis on healing rather than helping, on curing rather than caring. This goal is all right as long as healing is possible, but if it is not (as is true in most human situations) then an exclusive preoccupation with healing can only produce discouragement and frustration. Most of us need comfort in the midst of change. Most of us need to be supported and thereby empowered to endure tension and adversity, even as we continue to press for change. And all of us need to pray the prayer that in this day we wish were not true: "God grant me the serenity to accept the things I cannot change, courage to change the things I can, and wisdom to know the difference."

Death, then, teaches us to comfort because we cannot cure. Actually, we are talking about the inherent ambiguity of life—the fact that healing is not a simple possibility. Sometimes our preaching and our theology promote the idea that solutions are easy to come by. Recently, Walter Breuggeman reminded me of that fact when I heard him lecture on Isaiah. He pointed out that Isaiah tried to turn the Israelites from the gods of Babylon back to the God of Israel by maintaining that the gods of Babylon are mute and impotent while the Lord is active and powerful. It is understandable why Isaiah makes the contrast stark and absolute, but the more sober and agonizing question of faith is: "Is it true? Does the contrast correspond to our experience?" In many cases, the answer is no. Our situation and certainly our experience of God is often more ambiguous and more complex than that. The gods of Babylon are a temptation precisely because they do not seem mute and powerless. Sometimes, in fact, they seem more potent than God himself.

Our preaching and our theology may minimize the ambiguity, but our caring cannot. Our caring must deal with it, must acknowledge and come to terms with the fact that God at work in the ambiguities of history often seems ambiguous himself. We do not get instant results. Sometimes we cannot even change what we would like to change. Death epitomizes this stubborn fact, reinforcing the need for comfort and encouragement even as we strive for the healing of human relationships.

Death teaches a fourth and final lesson: A Christian understanding of death goes beyond our own demise and reminds us of Christ's death, of the supreme act of caring.

The previous three lessons are good as preconditions of caring, but it takes more than that to move us to care. We must first be cared for before we can care. In this sense, Christ defines the nature of our caring and is its source. He cared for us even when we did not care for him, and he continues to care for us in spite of our being difficult to care about. His care empowers us to care, not as a quality that we possess but as a response to his loving kindness.

In another chapter, I highlight the nature of Christian care by referring to Paul's metaphor of servant. That metaphor has obvious advantages to express the nature of our caring in a world of personal and interpersonal change. It indicates that our capacity to care is not rooted in our own being but that it depends upon our being cared for. If we do not live out of that love, then there is only anxiety—the anxiety of nonbeing manifested in the moral sphere as loss of one's destiny, in the spiritual sphere as loss of meaningful relationships, and in the ontic sphere as loss of one's life.

All of us are there! We have felt the tension of social upheaval and have felt more judged than cared for, more alienated than accepted. Our worry is not whether the lion will lie down with the calf. We are far from that biblical image. Our concern is whether spouse can find fulfillment in spouse, whether male and female can find peace between them, whether white and black can see each other as brothers and sisters. In a word, can we care for each other in the midst of changing relationships? I have tried to show that the awareness of death—the existential acknowledgment of our finitude—can instruct us in the art of caring. But most of all the awareness of death can lead us to Christ. He alone can empower us to care. And he alone can forgive us when we fail.

14

The Challenge of Becker:
A New Approach to Pastoral Care

LeRoy Aden

We are a mystery to ourselves. We look into a mirror and confront a reality that we cannot fathom. We try to capture ourselves in words and find that we are always more than the concepts and images that we use to describe ourselves.

On a behavioral level, we do things that make no apparent sense. We are tormented or inspired by a thought that we did not will. We are on the verge of a deep sleep and then suddenly are jerked back into consciousness by some vague but overpowering reality. Or in our sleep, we are disturbed by dreams that are so real and so terrifying that we wake up in a cold sweat.

Sigmund Freud tried to penetrate the mystery, and in the process he gave us a profound understanding of ourselves. He came to believe that all human behavior, even apparently meaningless behavior, has meaning. He means by this that all behavior has a cause, that there is a historical reason behind all of our thoughts and actions. For him, the reason resides in our desires or, more accurately, in the repression of our desires. Repressed desires operate as unconscious determinisms that influence and distort the present moment.

Freud's causal view of human striving has great explanatory power. It helps us to understand our irrational behaviors, including the doing of something we do not will, the sudden jerk from sleep to consciousness, the horrible dream that sends a chill through our being. It tells us that we are moved by unconscious forces as much as by conscious intentions.

For all of its profundity, Freud's theory is not fully satisfying, at least not for our pastoral ministry, because our malady is deeper and our reach is higher than his theory comprehends. Until recently, though, we have not had a psychological system that penetrates the mystery deep enough to lay bare its ultimate dimensions. Consequently, we adopted Freud's understanding, or even Carl R. Rogers's optimistic evaluation, of our human condition. Both approaches have made undeniable contributions to our pastoral care and counseling, but at the same time they have distorted our pastoral endeavor. They have taken us away from the root of the human problem and have tempted us to settle for penultimate answers to ultimate questions.

I believe we now have a psychology that sheds profound light on the mystery, the psychology of Ernest Becker. Becker, after experiencing the brutality of World War II firsthand, spent a lifetime trying "to peel away disguises and marginalia, trying to get at the truly basic things about man, the things that really drive him."[1] He studied and then taught in the United States in the area of cultural and social anthropology. He came to believe that what propels us as individuals is principally the fear of death, an idea that he developed in his Pulitzer-Prize winning book *The Denial of Death*. He was working on a sequel to this book when he found out that he had terminal cancer. He died in 1974 without finishing the manuscript, but his brilliant career was brought to a fitting close by the posthumous appearance of *The Escape from Evil*. These two books, along with Sam Keen's conversation with Becker a short time before his death, form the backdrop for this discussion on the application of Becker's insights to pastoral counseling.

Becker challenges Freud and especially Rogers at crucial points and gives us an understanding of our human condition that is compatible with our theological understanding of people. In the process, he turns the final reaches of pastoral care upside down. Under the influence of Rogers, pastoral care became primarily the art of comforting the afflicted. Its task was to rescue basically good individuals from a "natural—and tragic" distortion that occurred in infancy. Becker, while granting this distortion, locates evil on a deeper level, on the level of our own egoistic strivings. Thus he makes a place in pastoral care for afflicting the comfortable, for confronting us with our own self-centered attempt to secure life.

1. Ernest Becker, *The Escape from Evil* (New York: Free Press, 1975), 1.

This "new" direction for pastoral ministry deserves elaboration. I can begin by summarizing the core of Becker's thought.

The Drag of Creatureliness

With Reinhold Niebuhr, Becker maintains that we are children of both nature and spirit, a paradox of necessity and possibility. This means, on the one hand, that we have a temporal and spatial body that is subject to illness and eventually to death. We are limited and finite creatures who can never escape the need for food or air or warmth. In many different ways, we are subject to the laws and vicissitudes not only of physical causality but also of cultural and historical existence. On the other hand, we are children of the spirit. We have the power to stand above our surroundings and to fashion them according to our own desires. We can escape the barricades of our temporal existence and can imagine and pursue life under different circumstances or in a different age. We even have the freedom to stand outside of ourselves and to make ourselves the object of question or concern. We can contemplate our own death. Within limits, we can shape our own lives. In a word, we have the power of a god.

According to Becker, the paradox of god-likeness and worm-likeness sets up a distressing incongruity. We have the power to contemplate the mysteries of life, including the mystery that we ourselves are, and yet we live life and face death as vulnerable and impotent creatures who can be wiped out with a single blow. It is our creatureliness, our finite impotence that gets to us. For Becker, our creatureliness is epitomized in our body, especially by its anality. "Excreting is the curse that threatens madness because it shows man his abject finitude, his physicalness, the likely unreality of his hopes and dreams. But even more immediately, it represents man's utter bafflement at the sheer *non-sense* of creation."[2] The reach of the human imagination and the power of reflective thought are brought low by the demise of the body. Or we can spend years refining our skills and developing ourselves only to end up food for worms.

It is an impossible situation. As excreting, impotent creatures we cannot value ourselves very highly. As diseased and dying persons we know that we can never escape annihilation. So we are filled with fear or, as Becker prefers to say in order to convey its all-consuming nature, we are filled with *terror*. We long to live forever, but we know that we are condemned to die. The incongruity is too much. We must find a

---

2. Ernest Becker, *The Denial of Death* (New York: Free Press, 1973), 33.

solution in order to live with some sense of tranquility in the face of extinction.

We have the power to meet the challenge. We are not given a predetermined world where present and future are already set. Unlike animals of instinct, we are not determined by set perceptions or by preset responses. Instead we are impossible creatures, condemned to strive everlastingly to solve the riddle of life and death. We must create, or at least define, our own world of meaning, including the meaning that we ourselves have to ourselves and to others. Out of the givens of life, we must fabricate an existence that domesticates the terrifying paradox of the human condition—the paradox that we are god-like in our vision but worm-like in our mortality.

For Becker, the power to fabricate is a twofold power. It is, in the first instance, the power to repress, not just libidinal desires as in Freud but the terrifying aspects of both life and death. Repression "partializes" our situation, filtering out large chunks of it and thereby allowing us "to live decisively in an overwhelmingly miraculous and incomprehensible world, a world so full of beauty, majesty, and terror that if animals perceived it all they would be paralyzed to act."[3] According to Becker, we partialize by creating a particular style of life. We fashion, or at least adopt, a specific character, and this character narrows our perception of ourselves and the world. It serves as a buffer against our finite existence. Becker calls it a vital lie, that is, "a necessary and basic dishonesty about oneself and one's whole situation"[4] that allows us to live life with some degree of security and confidence.

The power to fabricate is, in the second instance, the power to inflate, to blow up our significance as a compensation for our powerlessness. Becker calls this fabrication the pursuit of the heroic, and as we will see he considers it the primary root of human evil. He maintains that we do not strive for ordinate significance but instead we seek to gain a sense of immortality, a sense of being of enduring and cosmic worth. We want "to earn a feeling of primary value, of cosmic specialness, of ultimate usefulness to creation, of unshakeable meaning,"[5] not necessarily on a global scale but within the orbit of our own life. We are driven to create the illusion that what we are or what we do will outlive us and that therefore we have succeeded in silencing the threat of death and decay.

According to Becker, each of us has individual ways to achieve immortality, but more generally culture offers codified and standardized

3. Ibid., 50.
4. Ibid., 55.
5. Ibid., 5.

opportunities. It has what is called hero-systems, prescribed means by which we can achieve a sense of lasting significance. In our capitalistic society, the accumulation of money is one of the chief means of immortality. It can be used to buy a variety of power-invested things. It can also be passed on to our successors and used to influence them. Thus it is "the human mode *par excellence* of coolly denying animal boundness, the determinism of nature."[6] But money is not the only symbol of immortality. Many other things can be invested with salutary power—the family, the state, the church. We sell our souls to one or more of these hero-systems, sacrificing freedom for the appearance of security against the terror of abject vulnerablity. We have "always casually sacrificed life for more life."[7]

The Root of Evil

As we have seen, Becker maintains that we use two primary means to deny our creatureliness: repression and self-inflation. He grants the necessity of the first one but finds great difficulty with the second one.

Repression is an absolutely necessary activity if we are to survive our incongruous situation. Unlike many of his humanistic colleagues, Becker does not posit a positive and self-actualizing core at the base of human life. Instead he sees an incurable tension, a paralyzing conflict between our creatureliness and our transcendence. The lifting of repression, then, does not bring a sense of fulfillment but an awesome and terrifying sense of conflict and impotence. Consequently, we must partialize and cut down the full stature of life in order to live with some semblance of tranquility. In fact, without represssion we would be driven mad by the sheer terror of our paradoxical situation and the overwhelming awesomeness of the world. For this reason Becker appreciates the value of repression, even though he also sees its crippling bind. It shrinks our vision and thus prevents us from having the full awareness that we need in order to actualize a more complete life.

Becker has a much more critical reaction to our tendency to inflate ourselves. He declares flatly that self-inflation is the "root cause of human evil," that it is not an innocent attitude that can be easily changed but is the basic and universal source of all human suffering. He explains: "Evil rests on the passionate personal motive to perpetuate oneself, and for each individual this is literally a life and death matter for which any sacrifice is not too great, provided it is the sac-

---

6. Becker, *Escape from Evil*, 82.
7. Ibid., 24.

rifice of someone else and provided that the leader and the group approve of it."[8]

Becker is concerned about the inordinacy of this drive, but he is even more concerned about its self-centeredness. To strive for immortality is to build on oneself. Becker's whole system says that we cannot live without illusions, but he believes just as strongly that our fabrications should not be centered in ourselves. Only "creative illusions," that is, only belief systems that transcend us and put us in contact with a power beyond ourselves, are salutary. For Becker, then, faith is essential to our sanity—in fact, to our very life, for without faith in a power beyond ourselves we stand naked before the full terror of life and death and are driven to sacrifice anyone whose decrease or demise might give us a sense of potence and immortality. Faith gets us beyond our own striving and links us with "the very ground of creation." Only then do we live with some sense of security in the face of our creatureliness.

Implications for Pastoral Care

Becker's understanding of our human conditions has at least two important implications for our pastoral attempt to help or to heal.

First, it redefines the basic human problem. As Rogers sees it, our predicament has to do with the denial or the distortion of a positive inner nature, resulting in a debilitating split between who we are and who we pretend to be. The goal of counseling, then, is to help the person become more whole by healing the split between surface and depth. Freud is more pessimistic about human nature, but he analyzes its disease in a similar way. The basic difficulty is repression, and thus the goal of therapeutic intervention is to lift the repressions and to free the individual of unconscious determinants. In both cases, pastoral care deals with historical enslavements, with paralyzing inner conflicts that people incur in the process of growing up. Both approaches imply that there are no deeper problems, no irreconcilable conflicts within human nature itself.

Becker's analysis puts the whole discussion on a different plane. He does not deny historical enslavements; in fact, he maintains that therapeutic psychology can be very helpful in freeing the individual from them. But he also recognizes that our predicament is deeper and less redeemable than Freud and especially Rogers would have us believe. He lifts out two characteristics of our plight that make it irreparable. First, he maintains that we are incurably cowards. Terrified by the awesomeness of life and the threat of death, we shut out large portions

8. Ibid., 122.

of each in order to gain some sense of peace and security. Second, he maintains that we are incurably idol-makers. We fabricate a world of meaning and significance in which we are like God. In the first instance, Becker extends Freud's concept of repression to the point of ultimate concern, to the point where we deny our creatureliness in order to appear invincible. In the second instance, Becker brings us to the threshold of sin, for he makes our predicament not just an early childhood split between surface and depth but a self-centered and inordinate attempt to make ourselves the center of the universe.

Becker's analysis puts our predicament beyond the range of psychotherapy. We can, and we must, take seriously the historical causes of our malady, but we must also realize that there is deeper trouble—trouble that cannot be resolved by our own resources. The flame of egoistic self-inflation burns brightly. And at this very point pastoral care and counseling needs to afflict us. It must bring a word of judgment to us, helping us to see through our immortality strivings and awakening the desire to move beyond them.

Second, Becker redefines the solution to our problem. He shows that increased self-knowledge, no matter how extensive, is not an adequate way out of our predicament. In fact, increased awareness of ourselves, which for Becker means increased knowledge of our incongruous creaturely nature, only increases our fear. It heightens the terrifying and paradoxical conflict that inheres in the human condition. Or as Becker says: The plunge into life can only bring into play "new and sharper paradoxes, new tensions, more painful disharmonies."[9] Thus the Freudian and Rogerian procedure of making conscious the unconscious will not do the trick, at least not by itself.

For Becker, increased self-awareness must lead beyond itself to faith. Self-analysis is valuable and necessary in the sense that it helps us to know and acknowledge our true condition, but the condition itself makes nothing less than faith a proper and healing response. By faith, Becker means giving ourselves over to a power beyond ourselves. He means that we transcend our egoistic attempts to become immortal and center our life in a God beyond the finite world. He uses Søren Kierkegaard to elaborate the point: "One goes through [the school of anxiety] to arrive at faith, the faith that one's very creatureliness has some meaning to a Creator; that despite one's true insignificance, weakness, death, one's existence has meaning in some ultimate sense because it exists within an eternal and infinite scheme of things brought about and maintained to some kind of design by some creative force."[10]

As a social scientist, Becker does not offer a detailed picture of God.

9. Becker, *The Denial of Death*, 281.
10. Ibid., 90.

He thinks that of all religions the Christian faith has achieved the best understanding of him, but he is not very explicit about its central affirmations or about his commitment to them. In fact, as Thomas A. Droege says, he is vague and disappointing at the very point that we look for answers. Of course, it is unrealistic, and even unfair, to expect a social scientist to fill in the gaps for us. What is astonishing is that he has shown us empirically the radical need for faith in a power beyond our human condition.

Pastoral care and counseling must take Becker's finding seriously. If he is correct, it means that faith, and not endless self-analysis, is the goal of our pastoral endeavor. For Christians, this means faith in a God who affirms our significance in the face of insignificance, our acceptance in the face of unacceptableness, our resurrection in the face of death. It means faith in a God who addresses and disarms Becker's most bitter truth—that we are vulnerable and impotent creatures who can spend a lifetime perfecting ourselves only to be wiped out with a single blow. The Christian faith rescues us from the devastation of this truth by its own truth. It affirms our creatureliness by positing a transcending ground for life that is not swallowed up by the finiteness of our being. It overcomes our own nonsignificance by affirming that we are of ultimate significance to God. And it transforms our mortality by making death the gateway to new life.

If faith in God is the end point of pastoral care, then pastoral care must be confessional and not simply analytical. It must testify to and mediate a power that transcends it infinitely, not by ignoring the concrete ways in which we pursue immortality but by dealing intensively with them. Becker gives us eyes to see. He exposes the constant and feverish presence of heroism, even when the outward appearance is one of underestimating the self or tranquilizing terror by immersing the self in trivia or participating in some other form of disguise. Pastoral care must examine this behavior and help individuals to see that they will never make it as long as they attempt to be the source of their own fulfillment. It must help them to grasp onto God, for by grasping onto him they grasp onto life from his side, opening themselves "up to infinity, to the possibility of cosmic heroism, to the very service of God."[11] This is the meaning of faith, and this is the meaning of life free from the terror of death.

Conclusion

We are a mystery to ourselves, and the greatest mystery of all is why we were created to die. We have no answer to this question, except

11. Ibid., 91.

the compulsive pursuit of our own immortality no matter whose life we must sacrifice. We have no answer, that is, unless we can hear the word of Christ: "For whoever would save his life will lose it, and whoever loses his life for my sake will find it" (Matt. 16:25).

Conclusion

The most healing insight for psychological theory and practice ever perceived by humans is the theological fact that God is for all of us and not against any of us, unconditionally. That biblical assertion, demonstrated by the long history of God's grace and providence in our lives, declares that God's forgiving and accepting grace is universal. Moreover, it describes his grace as of such a radical kind that it depends wholly upon God's character as gracious and forgiving God, and in no sense upon the quality of our characters as sinful and sick human beings.

Such grace is always a surprise to us who are accustomed to measuring our worth and value by how we measure up to standards of character and conduct that we imagine to be imposed upon us or that we impose upon ourselves. We have a built-in resistance to such radical, unconditional, and universal grace. It is almost unbelievable to all of us that we can be accepted, affirmed, and forgiven by God; loved and cherished by him, just as we are, without any strings attached.

We all prefer conditional grace, grace that requires us to do something—like confess our sins, change our ways, or ask God for his grace—before it can be dispensed to us. We prefer conditional grace for two reasons: first, that gives us control and perpetuates the fiction that we somehow have our hands on the levers that create our destiny; and second, so long as we can keep God's grace conditional we can justify conditional relationships with each other. We can continue to convey the impression that if others wish to have our approval, affirmation, kindness, caring, and love, they must be the right color, behave in the right way, go to the right church, hold their hats in their hands in the right fashion, and manifest the correct cultural and aesthetic sensitivities and goals. Conditional relationships are not cherishing or co-relative relationships but exploitive relationships. God's relationship to us is radical in the sense that it is co-relative and cherishing even when we are not cherishable, faithful and durable even when we are not faithful; forgiving and accepting of us as we are where we are. There is no other way to get beyond our defensiveness and our destructive need to always be measuring up to someone or something, thereby perpetually setting ourselves up for failure, guilt, diminished self-esteem, and perceived alienation from ourselves, each other, and God.

The authors of this volume have perceived this theological reality to be the foundation of all faith, life, and healing. They uniformly agree that this biblical revelation that first exploded in the mind of Abraham nearly four millennia ago is the precariously held mainstream of certainty in the believing community ever since. Moreover, the authors and editors have prepared this volume for the purpose of especially drawing out that implication of the biblical perspective that helps us see in various ways how God's grace, incarnated in the person and the perspective of the counselor, heals humans who are fractured by the neediness, shame, and inherent conflictedness of human experience.

So this book is intended to speak to pastoral psychology as a discipline, and to the pastoral counselor as a practitioner of the healing power of God and of the theology of his grace. This book also speaks to psychology as a discipline, and to the psychotherapist as a practitioner of the healing power of unconditional acceptance of fractured and needy persons who are caught in the travail of sickness and sin. It speaks of confrontation with our universal sense of inadequacy in view of the responsibilities of life and the challenges of godliness.

In our common human terror and our common hope, psychology has brought to us profound insights into the nature and function of our humanness, the ways and reasons our personalities grow or develop to health or sickness. The contemporary temptation among some evangelicals to denegrate the contributions of the science and discipline of psychology is an egregious and self-serving iconoclasm that should not be tolerated by thoughtful and serious scientists or practitioners. However, thoughtful and serious people in the helping professions of pastoring and psychotherapy should be just as intolerant of any ignorance of or insensitivity to the finite limits of psychology as a science or discipline. Although it lends us invaluable insights into human personality dynamics in sickness and health, psychology has not been able to completely account for or explore the mysterious reaches of our humanness. One prominent dimension of the psyche that psychology seems persistently ill-equipped to investigate in a satisfactory way and to an adequate degree is the spiritual dimension of our selfhood.

That spiritual dimension is the function of the human psyche, which expresses our inherent and irrepressible need to reach out to meaning, to stand in awe of the "sense of the holy," to bond in durable and life-enhancing relationships, to transcend the pervasive wrongness and mystification of reality and place ourselves in postures of appropriateness and wholesomeness before the face of others and of God, to be true to ourselves with a sense of deep inner authenticity, and to love God and find our true selves in his love for us. Exploration of that spiritual dimension of humanness is the task and opportunity of the science and discipline of theology, and it is faith's long quest.

Thus it is that this book affirms psychology but insists upon the urgency of sound theology and comprehensive theological method, not just in the speculative fields of philosophical reflections on dogma, but especially in the field of pastoral care and the contributions it brings to the practical issues of human healing. Indeed, we have been intentional in our emphasis that in the theory and practice of pastoral care (pastoral theology, pastoral psychology, pastoral counseling, clinical pastoral education, and related disciplines) pastoral theology is paramount.

Each author has carried forward that thesis as it applies to each of the specific aspects he addressed. This conscious design arises from a sense of urgency about building the future of pastoral care in and through the church in a direction that will root it once again in the dynamic insights of biblical theology, rather than in mere secular psychology. So this book looks toward the future. It hopes to carry the enterprise of human healing deeper, and with a keener focus, into the spiritual depths of human fracturedness, as well as into the mysterious depths of the heart and life of God with his people. It does not conceive of itself as an ending, but as the midwife of a new beginning in which pastoral care becomes a vital dimension of our Christian faith and an essential function of our Christian ministry.

Bibliography

Adams, Jay E. *Competent to Counsel.* Nutley, N.J.: Presbyterian and Reformed, 1970.

————— . *The Use of the Scriptures in Counseling.* Grand Rapids: Baker, 1975.

Aden, LeRoy. "Faith and the Developmental Cycle." *Pastoral Psychology* 24 (1976): 215–30.

————— . "On Carl Rogers' Becoming." *Theology Today* 36, no. 4 (January 1980): 556–59.

Anderson, Herbert. *The Family and Pastoral Care.* Philadelphia: Fortress, 1984.

————— . "The Death of a Parent: Its Impact on Middle-Aged Sons and Daughters." *Pastoral Psychology* 28 (Spring 1980): 151–67.

Angyal, Andras. *Neurosis and Treatment: A Holistic Theory.* New York: Wiley and Sons, 1965.

Barnhouse, Ruth. "Spiritual Direction and Psychotherapy." *Journal of Pastoral Care* 33 (September 1979): 149–63.

Becker, Ernest. *The Denial of Death.* New York: Free Press, 1973.

————— . *The Escape from Evil.* New York: Free Press, 1975.

Boisen, Anton. *Explorations of the Inner World.* New York: Harper, 1936.

————— . *Out of the Depths.* New York: Harper, 1960.

Bonhoeffer, Dietrich. *Ethics.* Edited by Eberhard Bethge. New York: Macmillan, 1955.

————— . *Letters and Papers from Prison.* Translated by Reginald H. Fuller. New York: Macmillan, 1953.

Borg, Marcus. "Death as the Teacher of Wisdom." *The Christian Century* 103 (February 26, 1986): 203–6.

191

Bornkamm, Gunther. *The New Testament: A Guide to Its Writings.* New ed. Translated by Reginald H. and Ilse Fuller. Philadelphia: Fortress, 1973.

Brigdes, Charles. *The Christian Ministry.* New York: Carter, 1847.

Browning, Don S. *Atonement and Psychotherapy.* Philadelphia: Westminster, 1966.

————. *The Moral Context of Pastoral Care.* Philadelphia: Westminster, 1976.

————. *Religious Ethics and Pastoral Care.* Philadelphia: Fortress, 1983.

Burnet, Gilbert. *A Discourse of the Pastoral Care.* 1692. London: Baynes, 1818.

Cabot, Richard C., and Russell L. Dicks. *The Art of Ministering to the Sick.* New York: Macmillan, 1936.

Campbell, Alastair V. *Rediscovering Pastoral Care.* Philadelphia: Westminster, 1981.

Capps, Donald. *Biblical Approaches to Pastoral Counseling.* Philadelphia: Westminster, 1981.

————. *Life Cycle Theory and Pastoral Care.* Philadelphia: Fortress, 1983.

————. *Pastoral Care and Hermeneutics.* Philadelphia: Fortress, 1984.

Carter, Elizabeth A., and Monica McGoldrick, editors. *The Family Life Cycle: A Framework for Family Therapy.* New York: Gardner, 1980.

Carter, John D., and Bruce Narramore. *The Integration of Psychology and Theology: An Introduction.* Grand Rapids: Zondervan, 1979.

Clebsch, William A., and Charles R. Jaekle. *Pastoral Care in Historical Perspective.* Englewood Cliffs: Prentice-Hall, 1964.

Clinebell, Howard. *Basic Types of Pastoral Counseling.* Nashville: Abingdon, 1966.

Cobb, John B., Jr. *Theology and Pastoral Care.* Philadelphia: Fortress, 1977.

Coenen, Lothar. "Proclamation, Preach, Kerygma." Pp. 54–57 in *The New International Dictionary of New Testament Theology,* vol. 3, edited by Colin Brown. Grand Rapids: Zondervan, 1978.

Collins, Gary R. *Effective Counseling.* Carol Stream, Ill.: Creation House, 1972.

————. *Psychology and Theology: Prospects for Integration.* Edited by H. Newton Malony. Nashville: Abingdon, 1981.

Droege, Thomas A. "A Developmental View of Faith." *Journal of Religion and Health* 3 (1974): 313–29.

————. *Self-Realization and Faith.* River Forest, Ill.: Lutheran Education Association, 1978.

Elert, Werner. *The Structure of Lutheranism.* Translated by W. A. Hansen. Saint Louis: Concordia, 1962.

Ellens, J. Harold. "Biblical Themes in Psychological Theory and Practice." *The Bulletin* 6, no. 2 (1980): 2–6.

————. *God's Grace and Human Health.* Nashville: Abingdon, 1982.

Emerson, J. G. *The Dynamics of Forgiveness.* Philadelphia: Westminster, 1964.

Erikson, Erik H. *Childhood and Society.* New York: Norton, 1963.

————. *Identity and the Life Cycle.* New York: International Universities Press, 1959.

————. *Insight and Responsibility.* New York: Norton, 1964.

Fairbairn, Patrick. *Pastoral Theology.* Edinburgh: T. and T. Clark, 1872.

Fowler, James W. *Life Maps: Conversations on the Journey of Faith.* Waco: Word, 1978.

————. *Stages of Faith.* New York: Harper and Row, 1981.

Freud, Sigmund. *The Ego and the Id.* Translated by Joan Riviere. London: Hogarth, 1927.

Gerkin, Charles V. *Crisis Experience in Modern Life.* Nashville: Abingdon, 1979.

————. *The Living Human Document.* Nashville: Abingdon, 1983.

Gladden, Washington. *The Christian Pastor.* New York: Charles Scribner's Sons, 1898.

Groeschel, Benedict J. *Spiritual Passages.* New York: Crossroad, 1983.

Groome, Thomas. *Christian Religious Education.* New York: Harper and Row, 1980.

Halpern, Howard M. *Cutting Loose: An Adult Guide to Dealing with Your Parents.* New York: Simon and Schuster, 1976.

Hartmann, Heinz. *Psychoanalysis and Moral Values.* New York: International Universities Press, 1960.

Hiltner, Seward. *Christian Shepherd.* Nashville: Abingdon, 1959.

————. *Pastoral Counseling.* Nashville: Abingdon, 1949.

————. *Preface to Pastoral Theology.* Nashville: Abingdon, 1958.

————. *Theological Dynamics.* Nashville: Abingdon, 1972.

————, ed. *Clinical Pastoral Training.* New York: Federal Council of Churches, 1945.

Hiltner, Seward, and Lowell G. Colston. *The Context of Pastoral Counseling.* Nashville: Abingdon, 1961.

Holifield, E. B. *A History of Pastoral Care in America.* Nashville: Abingdon, 1983.

Hoppin, James M. *Pastoral Theology.* New York: Funk and Wagnalls, 1884.

Horney, Karen. *Neurosis and Human Growth: The Struggle Toward Self-Realization.* New York: Norton, 1950.

Johnson, Cedric B. *The Psychology of Biblical Interpretation.* Grand Rapids: Zondervan, 1983.

Joy, Donald M., and others. *Moral Development Foundations, Judeo-Christian Alternatives to Piaget/Kohlberg.* Nashville: Abingdon, 1983.

Kemp, Charles. *Physicians of the Soul: A History of Pastoral Counseling.* New York: Macmillan, 1947.

Kerr, Hugh T., and John M. Mulder. *Conversions.* Grand Rapids: Eerdmans, 1983.

Kidder, Daniel. *The Christian Pastorate.* New York: Methodist Book Concern, 1871.

Koestlin, Heinrich. *Die Lehre von der Seelsorge.* Berlin: Reuther and Reichard, 1895.

————— . "Moral Stages and Moralization." Pp. 31–53 in *Moral Development and Behavior,* edited by T. Lickona. New York: Holt, Rinehart and Winston, 1976.

Kopp, Sheldon B. *If You Meet the Buddha on the Road, Kill Him.* Palo Alto, Calif.: Science and Behavior, 1972.

Kübler-Ross, Elisabeth. *On Death and Dying.* New York: Macmillan, 1969.

Lake, Frank. *Clinical Theology.* London: Darton, Longman and Todd, 1966.

Levinson, Daniel J., and others. *The Seasons of a Man's Life.* New York: Knopf, 1978.

Loder, James E. *The Transforming Moment.* New York: Harper and Row, 1981.

Luther, Martin. "The Freedom of a Christian." Pp. 327–77 in *Luther's Works,* vol. 31. Philadelphia: Muhlenberg, 1957.

Massey, J. E. *You Are Where You Were When.* Videotape series. Boulder, Colo.

McNeill, John T. *A History of the Cure of Souls.* New York: Harper, 1951.

Menninger, Karl. *Whatever Became of Sin?* New York: Hawthorn, 1972.

Minuchin, Salvador. *Families and Family Therapy.* Cambridge: Harvard University Press, 1974.

Mitchell, Kenneth, and Herbert Anderson. "You Must Leave Before You Can Cleave: A Family Systems Approach to Premarital Pastoral Work." *Pastoral Psychology* 30 (Winter 1981): 71–88.

Moran, Gabriel. *Religious Educational Developmental.* Minneapolis: Winston, 1983.

Mowrer, O. Hobart. *The Crisis in Psychiatry and Religion.* New York: Van Nostrand, 1961.

Napier, Augustus, and Carl Whitiker. *The Family Crucible.* New York: Harper and Row, 1978.

Nelson, James B. *Between Two Gardens: Reflections on Sexuality and Religious Experience.* New York: Pilgrim, 1983.

Niebuhr, Reinhold. *The Nature and Destiny of Man.* New York: Charles Scribner's Sons, 1953.

Noyce, Gaylord. *The Art of Pastoral Conversation.* Atlanta: John Knox, 1981.

Nuttin, Joseph. *Psychoanalysis and Personality.* New York: New American Library, 1962.

Oates, Wayne E. *The Bible in Pastoral Care.* Philadelphia: Westminster, 1953.

————. *Pastoral Counseling.* Philadelphia: Westminster, 1974.

————. *The Psychology of Religion.* Waco: Word, 1973.

Oden, Thomas C. *Care of Souls in the Classic Tradition.* Philadelphia: Fortress, 1984.

————. *Contemporary Theology and Psychotherapy.* Philadelphia: Westminster, 1967.

————. *Game Free: A Guide to the Meaning of Intimacy.* New York: Harper and Row, 1974.

————. *Guilt Free.* Nashville: Abingdon, 1980.

————. *Pastoral Theology: Essentials of Ministry.* San Francisco: Harper and Row, 1983.

————. *The Structure of Awareness.* New York: Abingdon, 1969.

Oglesby, William B., Jr. *Biblical Themes for Pastoral Care.* Nashville: Abingdon, 1980.

Pascal, Blaise. *Pensées and Provincial Letters.* New York: Modern Library, 1941.

Peterson, Eugene. *Five Smooth Stones for Pastoral Work.* Atlanta: John Knox, 1980.

Piaget, Jean. *The Psychology of the Child.* New York: Random, 1969.

————. *Six Psychological Studies.* New York: Random, 1967.

Pruyser, Paul W. *The Minsister as Diagnostician.* Philadelphia: Westminster, 1976.

Rhodes, Sonya, with Josleen Wilson. *Surviving Family Life: The Seven Crises of Living Together.* New York: Putnam, 1981.

Ricoeur, Paul. "Toward a Hermeneutic of the Idea of Revelation." Pp. 73–118 in *Essays on Biblical Interpretation*, edited by Lewis C. Mudge. Philadelphia: Westminster, 1980.

Rogers, Carl R. *On Becoming a Person: A Therapist's View of Psychotherapy.* Boston: Houghton Mifflin, 1961.

Sailer, Jacob. *Vorlseungen aus der Pastoraltheologie.* Munich: Lentner, 1788.

Satir, Virginia M. *Peoplemaking.* Palo Alto, Calif.: Science and Behavior, 1972.

Schneider, Carl D. "Faith Development and Pastoral Diagnosis." Pp. 221–50 in *Faith Development and Fowler*, edited by Craig Dykstra and Sharon Parks. Birmingham, Ala.: Religious Education Press, 1986.

Shedd, William G. T. *Homiletics and Pastoral Theology.* New York: Charles Scribner's Sons, 1867.

Smedes, Lewis B. *Forgive and Forget.* New York: Harper and Row, 1984.

Stahmann, Robert F., and William J. Hiebert. *Premarital Counseling.* Lexington, Mass.: Heath, 1980.

Stollberg, Dietrich. *Therapeutische Seelsorge.* Munich: Chr. Kaiser, 1969.

Switzer, David K. *Pastor, Preaching, Person: Developing a Pastoral Ministry in Depth.* Nashville: Abingdon, 1979.

Thielicke, Helmut. *Death and Life.* Translated by Edward H. Schroeder. Philadelphia: Fortress, 1970.

Thornton, Edward. *Professional Education for Ministry: A History of Clinical Pastoral Education.* Nashville: Abingdon, 1969.

Thurneysen, Eduard. *A Theology of Pastoral Care.* Translated by Jack A. Worthington and Thomas Wieser. Atlanta: John Knox, 1962.

Tillich, Paul. *The Courage to Be.* New Haven: Yale University Press, 1952.

————— . *The Dynamics of Faith.* New York: Harper and Row, 1957.

————— . *Morality and Beyond.* New York: Harper and Row, 1963.

Tournier, Paul. *The Doctor's Casebook in the Light of the Bible.* New York: Harper, 1960.

Vitz, Paul. *Psychology as Religion.* Grand Rapids: Eerdmans, 1977.

Westerhof, John. *Will Our Children Have Faith?* New York: Seabury, 1976.

Williams, Daniel Day. *The Minister and the Care of Souls.* New York: Harper and Row, 1961.

Wise, Carroll A. *Pastoral Counseling.* New York: Harper, 1951.

————— . *Psychiatry and the Bible.* New York: Harper and Row, 1956.

Wuellner, Wilhelm H., and Robert C. Leslie. *The Surprising Gospel.* Nashville: Abingdon, 1984.

Index of Authors
and Subjects